Praise for Working People**Smart**

"Working People**Smart** belongs in every workplace. Not only should it be required reading, it should be required *doing*. Work life would be a whole lot more fun, fulfilling, and fruitful if we'd all implement the six strategies that Mel Silberman and Freda Hansburg so masterfully present in this wonderfully useful book. I assure you that when you put in practice even one of their coaching tips, you'll immediately notice results. And Working People**Smart** should also come with a warning label that reads: *Try this at home. Your family will love you for it.*"

–Jim Kouzes, coauthor of *The Leadership Challenge* and *Encouraging the Heart,* and Chairman Emeritus, Tom Peters Company

"Working People**Smart** is a must-read for individuals who deal with a variety of challenging interpersonal interactions every day! Applying practical, real-world approaches, Mel and Freda provide an insightful and practical look at how to improve your personal impact and effectiveness in the workplace."

–Richard Chang, CEO, Richard Chang Associates, Inc., and author of *The Passion Plan* and *The Passion Plan at Work*

"Time and time again, business success comes back to how people relate to each other. That's why BMW has been conducting 'Working People**Smart**' seminars for the past two years and using the book People**Smart** to improve the interpersonal intelligence of its employees. With the publication of **Working PeopleSmart**, we now have the field manual for making the concepts of **PeopleSmart** work. Its real-world advice and business-related scenarios offer an exceptionally clear pathway to put these strategies into action."

> —Viki Macdonald, BMW Group University, BMW of North America, LLC

"**Working PeopleSmart** could well be called a guidebook for everyday living in the workplace, providing strategies, practice scenarios, and tips for handling virtually all of the interpersonal issues that occur daily in corporate America. This book is a must-have for new professionals entering the workforce for the first time, for the new supervisor, and for seasoned leaders who desire to continuously increase and broaden their influence, trust, and communication skills."

> —Doris M. Sims, SPHR, Leadership Development Director, *AdvancePCS*, and author of *Creative New Employee Orientation Programs*

"If common sense were common, we wouldn't need Silberman and Hansburg's wonderfully clear, cogent and imaginative guidelines to interpersonal communication. Their six basic strategies for managing workplace communication—with bosses, coworkers, customers—are aptly designed to make one's job not only more effective but one's life more pleasant, as well."

> —George David Smith, Academic Director, Executive Programs, NYU Stern School of Business

Working

People**Smart**

Working
PeopleSmart

6 Strategies for Success

Mel Silberman, Ph.D.
Freda Hansburg, Ph.D.

BERRETT-KOEHLER PUBLISHERS, INC.
San Francisco

Berrett-Koehler Publishers, Inc.
235 Montgomery Street, Suite 650
San Francisco, CA 94104-2916
Tel: (415)288-0260   Fax: (415) 326-2512 www.bkconnection.com

Ordering Information
Quantity sales. Special discounts are available on quantity purchases by corporations, associations, and others. For details, contact the "Special Sales Department" at the Berrett-Koehler address above.
Individual sales. Berrett-Koehler publications are available through most bookstores. They can also be ordered direct from Berrett-Koehler: Tel: (800) 929-2929; Fax: (802) 864-7626; www.bkconnection.com
Orders for college textbook/course adoption use. Please contact Berrett-Koehler: Tel: (800) 929-2929; Fax: (802) 864-7626.
Orders for U.S. trade bookstores and wholesalers. Please contact Publishers Group West, 1700 Fourth Street, Berkeley, CA 94710. Tel: (510) 528-1444; Fax (5510) 528-3444.

Berrett-Koehler and the BK logo are registered trademarks of Berrett-Koehler Publishers, Inc. Printed in the United States of America

Berrett-Koehler books are printed on long-lasting acid-free paper. When it is available, we choose paper that has been manufactured by environmentally responsible processes. These may include using trees grown in sustainable forests, incorporating recycled paper, minimizing chlorine in bleaching, or recycling the energy produced at the paper mill.

Project Manager: Susie Yates, Publication Services, Inc.
Supervising Editor: Dave Mason, Publication Services, Inc.
Project Coordinator: James Auler, Publication Services, Inc.
Design: Foti Kutil, Publication Services, Inc.
Layout: Dorothy Evans, Steve Sansone, Publication Services, Inc.

Library of Congress Cataloging-in-Publication Data
Silberman, Melvin L.
    Working peoplesmart : 6 strategies for success / Mel Silberman, Freda Hansburg.
      p. cm.
    Includes bibliographical references and index.
    ISBN 1-57675-208-9
    1. Psychology, Industrial--Handbooks, manuals, etc. 2. Success in business--Handbooks, manuals, etc. 3. Interpersonal relations--Handbooks, manuals, etc. 4. Organizational effectiveness--Handbooks, manuals, etc. I. Hansburg, Freda, 1950- II. Title.

HF5548.8S518 2004
650.1'3--dc22   2003063868

First Edition
08 07 06 05 04   10 9 8 7 6 5 4 3 2 1

Contents

4-27-05

Strategy 3: Speak Up (with Tact)
Rather than Suffer in Silence 69

Strategy 4: Invite Others to Be Your Mirror
Rather than Your Blind Spot 99

Strategy 5: Be Open to Resistance
Rather than Fight It 127

Preface

Interpersonal tensions have business consequences! The purpose of this book is to lessen these tensions so that you and the organization in which you are employed can be more successful—regardless of what business you are in.

What you will discover in *Working PeopleSmart* is your own personal coaching guide to improving your relationship with everyone with whom you work. That includes your colleagues and customers, the employees you may supervise, and even your boss! It's a book you can pull down from your shelf to obtain instant advice whenever you want.

Since the publication of our book *PeopleSmart*, we have been conducting "Working PeopleSmart" seminars with a wide variety of businesses and organizations. They have included major corporations, small companies, nonprofits, and educational institutions. We've also trained at every level—senior and mid-level managers, front-line supervisors, and support personnel. In each case, we are there to develop the organization's capacity to build positive, productive relationships within its workforce.

Six strategies for success have emerged from these three years of consulting and training. This book will explain how to leverage each strategy for your own professional success.

And there is more.

As we take participants through the principles and practices of working people-smart, we invite them to tell us the people problems they experience. As a result of this process, we have been privy to a bumper crop of challenging situations. In *Working PeopleSmart*, we have captured the most vexing questions posed to us and provided our people-smart advice. We hope that you, the reader, will gain a greater awareness of the options you have for handling tough situations and will be inspired to try some of them.

Reading advice is never enough. You must try out the advice and see if it works for you. Granted, it takes some courage to do something different, to think and act "outside the box." If you are willing, you will be rewarded with greater confidence and the ability to bring out the best in even the worst of circumstances.

There are tangible rewards for you as well. If you have the skills to bring out the best in others, you will be an invaluable resource in your organization. As a result, your people talents will be recognized and you will be more likely to succeed in your career.

One of the things we have learned ourselves as we attempt to work people-smart is that success is achieved only when you cultivate "partners." In compiling this book, we benefited from several partners and would like to acknowledge them.

We thank the many "Working PeopleSmart" seminar sponsors and participants for your candor, your courage, and your enthusiastic acceptance of our training approach.

We appreciate the exceptional talents of our PeopleSmart Consultant Network, a group of professionals around the country who have brought "Working PeopleSmart" seminars to a greater audience than we could by ourselves.

Our publishing partner, Berrett-Koehler (and especially its president, Steve Piersanti), has been very supportive of our work. BK is the most author-friendly publisher one could ever find.

Finally, we are grateful to our life partners, Shoshana and Dan, for their abundant love and faith in our PeopleSmart endeavors.

Mel Silberman, Princeton, NJ

Freda Hansburg, Berkeley Heights, NJ

March 2004

Introduction

Bringing out the best in others is good business.

When we bring both respect and interpersonal savvy to our work relationships, we do more than make people feel good. We enhance personal and organizational performance. Customers are more likely to return to companies that treat them well. Staff show more loyalty to supportive employers. Cohesive teams are more productive. Individuals with strong people skills are more likely to succeed–and far less likely to be fired.

As the workplace grows more complex and competitive, managing our work relationships becomes even more essential *and* difficult. Today's challenges in organizational life include:

Doing more with less–enhancing productivity and collaboration among teams with depleted numbers and morale

Bringing people together–bridging the gaps posed by diversity and virtual workplaces to promote understanding and effective communication

Building leadership–developing managers who bring out the best in their people, rather than put out fires among them

All of these situations pose daily interpersonal dilemmas as we deal with customers, colleagues, supervisors, and people who may report to us. Unfortunately, for many of us the workplace is not an interpersonal bed of roses. Tensions among co-workers are increasing. In one recent survey nearly 70% of people at work reported themselves the victims of rudeness and put-downs from fellow workers–and they retaliated by bad-mouthing the company, missing deadlines, and treating customers disrespectfully.* Does this sound like something you've experienced?

We believe that the worst way to respond to these mounting interpersonal tensions is by retaliating, despairing, or becoming cynical. These reactions only perpetuate the negativity. The only way out of the morass is to work people-smart. What's more, we believe that anyone can. Our goal in this book is to demonstrate how you

---

*Lisa Penney, reported in *APA MONITOR,* vol. 34, No. 6, June 2003, p.11.

can face the most daunting interpersonal scenarios and turn them into opportunities for success, using six key strategies.

What Is "Working People-Smart"?

Individuals who work people-smart focus on bringing out the best in others on the job. They know how to open people up rather than make them defensive or resistant. They have a knack for defusing tension rather than creating it. They set a good example through their own behavior and can inspire and influence those with weaker skills.

What does it take to work people-smart?

As we described in our previous book, *PeopleSmart: Developing Your Interpersonal Intelligence,* being savvy with people is a multifaceted competence that includes eight core skills:

❑ Understanding people

❑ Expressing yourself clearly

❑ Asserting your needs

❑ Seeking and giving feedback

❑ Influencing others

❑ Resolving conflict

❑ Being a team player

❑ Shifting gears when relationships are stuck

Mastering all eight of these skills is a lifetime effort. Few of us are fortunate enough to have been born with interpersonal genius. Most of us need to work at it. But the good news is that all of us can improve our interpersonal intelligence by applying the suggestions provided in *PeopleSmart*. The book serves as a personal training guide to be used in any life situation in which bringing out the best in others is imperative.

Since the publication of *PeopleSmart,* we've learned more about the essential ingredients of being people-smart—especially as it applies to the workplace. Our consulting assignments have brought us to a wide variety of work environments. We've observed individuals at all levels and in different environments, such as large corporations, nonprofit organizations, government agencies, small businesses, and educational institutions. We have paid particular attention to the four key arenas in which strong people skills are critical:

- ❑ Relating to your boss
- ❑ Supervising and coaching others
- ❑ Collaborating with colleagues and teammates
- ❑ Serving or selling to customers

As a result of this opportunity, we have identified six "strategies" that separate the person who works people-smart from those who do not. We call them "strategies" because they go beyond "skills." They are the basic approaches people take with others that allow them to succeed in key relationships . . . and garner success.

In *Working PeopleSmart,* we will explore each of these strategies for success. We'll look at how and why people-smart individuals employ them, especially in tough situations. Here are the six strategies of working people-smart.

Six Strategies for Success

Strategy ① Be Curious Rather than Furious

When interacting with a myriad of people, we inevitably experience some of them as challenging or difficult to understand. Often, this upsetting experience leads to frustration and sometimes anger. Those who work people-smart make it a practice to understand the challenging behaviors of others instead of just getting upset.

Strategy ② Include the Listener Rather than Talk at Him or Her

When we communicate information to others, our messages may be unclear because we fail to think about the needs of the listener. Those who work people-smart have figured out that the listener is their "communication partner." They make it a practice to consider the listener's frame of reference and foster two-way communication exchanges that increase understanding.

Strategy ③ — Speak Up (with Tact) Rather than Suffer in Silence

All of us experience moments at work when we should express our own views, needs, and expectations to others. Some of us remain silent and resentment builds. Others of us speak up for ourselves without hesitation but do so in ways that make others defensive. Those who work people-smart understand that their own ideas and concerns are important, and they make it their business to express them in ways that are clear but respectful of others.

Strategy ④ — Invite Others to Be Your Mirror Rather than Your Blind Spot

Other people have perspectives about our performance that are useful to our growth and development. However, most of us are reluctant to seek feedback from those with whom we work. Those who work people-smart understand that "feedback is the breakfast of champions." They seek the feedback of others rather than wait for it, and they develop strategies that encourage constructive feedback.

Strategy ⑤ — Be Open to Resistance Rather than Fight It

People at work don't always agree with each other or follow each other's recommendations. All too often, when faced with disagreement or conflict, people become either argumentative or avoiding. Those who work people-smart are influential because they consistently "surface" resistance by making efforts to understand the concerns and objections of others and use that information to build agreement and resolution.

Teamwork is essential in any organization. Often, we act in ways that don't contribute to teamwork—without even realizing it. Although our intentions may not be selfish, our actions wind up serving only ourselves. Those who work people-smart gain from behaviors that foster collaborative rather than individual effort.

Can I Work People-Smart?

By now you may be asking yourself, "*Can I do all that?*" Our answer is a resounding yes. As psychologists, we have seen time and again that people can and do change—given two conditions:

You must *decide* to change. You are the one who has to take the initiative to turn things around. Makeovers may happen on "reality" TV, but in real life we can't change other people. The best we can do is change ourselves. Fortunately, by doing this, we often elicit something new from others.

You must *work* at change. Our six strategies are long-term endeavors, not quick fixes. This is not to say that a single people-smart response *won't* transform a bad situation. It often does. But you will have to be patient and persistent at integrating the strategies into your daily life, and not abandon your efforts when you encounter setbacks.

If you need some help applying these strategies, we are here to serve as your virtual coach and guide you through difficult work relationships skillfully and gracefully. Everyone encounters interpersonal situations that test the capacity to be people-smart. After describing each of the six strategies of working people-smart, we will look at such dilemmas—the challenging, realistic scenarios that test your people skills—and offer our people-smart prescriptions for handling them effectively. We'll provide coaching tips for each scenario and let you hear exactly what a people-smart response sounds like.

So here is the coaching contract we propose.

We will share the know-how you require to sharpen your people edge. Your job will be to take these strategies to work with you. Are you ready to begin?

Strategy 1:

Be Curious Rather than Furious

We all know people who challenge our ability to work people-smart. Do any of these "challengers" sound familiar to you?

Among customers, you might find "Carol Complainer": *"Is this the best you can do?"*

Or "Harvey Hierarchy": *"What's the name of your supervisor?"*

Among co-workers, you might find "Needy Nan": *"Can you help me out?" "Want to hear about my weekend?"* Or "Superior Stan": *"Mistakes? I never make any . . . unlike you!"*

Among direct reports, you might find "Late Nate": *"No, it was yesterday that the bus was late. Today, I had to take my son to the dentist."* Or "Pathetic Patty": *"I can't do this! You'll have to show me how."*

Finally, your boss might be like "Ted Tyrant": *"I'd rather be right than loved!"*

Or "Carla Cryptic": *"I don't have time to go over this. Just figure it out yourself."*

When people at work engage in such unpleasant behavior, it's only human to be annoyed or even furious. Typically, we might cope by doing any or all of the following:

❑ Avoid them whenever possible.

❑ Complain about them to a trusted colleague.

❑ Write them off as people who can't or won't change their ways.

❑ Respond in kind by being equally unpleasant.

As much as any of these challenging people at work may frustrate us, the people-smart thing to do is get curious as to *why* they act the way they do rather than merely get upset about *what* they do. This involves trying to develop an "empathetic understanding" of a person who is puzzling. What is it like to be in this person's shoes?

You may not like or approve of the other person's behavior. Certainly, no one should tolerate irresponsible behavior. Nonetheless, it pays to explore why the person acts the way he or she does.

❑ It may unlock new ways to relate to the person that will be productive for both of you.

❑ It may give you a new perspective on the person, help you get some distance, and avoid taking what the person does too personally.

❑ It may win the appreciation of that person and serve as the basis for a better relationship.

In contrast, failing to explore the possible causes of the person's behavior not only perpetuates the impasse but also leads to increasing frustration and, ultimately, cynicism. When we accumulate a list of too many "hopeless cases," we may become even quicker to write people off and find ourselves walled off from others.

Let's look at an example of how "furious" might begin shifting to "curious."

In the accounting office where I work as office manager, there is an accountant named Helen, who couldn't be more different from me. She always seems down in the dumps, grumbling under her breath and looking angry. She doesn't respond to jokes and never joins the rest of us in the lunchroom. She just focuses on her work and keeps reminding everybody how much responsibility she has.

I'm a much more social person. I always get my work done, but I also like to talk with people throughout the day, pass along humorous stories via e-mail, and so forth. If we were two of the seven dwarfs, I'd be Happy and Helen would be Grumpy. I know we also have significant differences in our personal lives. Helen is a single mother, living with her elderly parents in their home, both of whom have had some serious health problems. I am married and live with my husband and two of my three young adult daughters in our own home.

Have I written off Helen? I guess if I were in her shoes, I'd feel overwhelmed with responsibilities. Raising a child alone, caring for elderly parents, and then coming to a job where she's trying to help fatten other people's bankrolls, when she doesn't even own a home . . . that's pretty bleak. If I were in survival mode like Helen, some of the stuff I talk about, and certainly many of the e-mail jokes I circulate, would probably look pretty superficial.

What really prompted me to reconsider my attitude toward Helen was an office crisis. Someone made a mistake and overlooked an important deadline with one of the accounts. It was Helen who caught the error in time to request an extension. I still wouldn't want to live with my nose to the grindstone the way she does, but maybe she has a point about responsibility. It rocks my boat to think that perhaps I've been a bit smug in my attitude toward her.

Although she hasn't become Helen's buddy, the office manager has taken a crucial step forward in their relationship. By walking in Helen's shoes for a few paces, and accepting the possibility that Helen's differences aren't necessarily all deficits, she has opened the door just enough to gain a small glimpse of who may be on the other side.

Five Coaching Tips to Understand Other People Better

Whenever we become frustrated by another person at work, that frustration can eat away at our energy to perform at our best. The good news is that we have several opportunities to "become curious rather than furious."

> **(1) Take time to listen to this person.**

When this challenging person talks, give him or her your full attention, without "running your own tape" about what you'll say next. Try to avoid interrupting what he or she is saying or simply tuning the person out. You might even paraphrase what you hear the person saying, so that he or she gets the idea that you're really listening.

Undoubtedly, you've heard much of what the person is about to tell you before. People have a tendency to repeat themselves. We all have "stump speeches," much like politicians. However, if you encourage the person to keep talking, he or she might go beyond the usual "stump speech" and tell you things he or she has never said before. That's when you begin to get the information to help you really understand where this person is coming from. You must make a clear decision that the other person is someone worth listening to and give him or her your full concentration. Imagine a spotlight shining on the speaker. If you are doing something else that could distract you, stop. Instead of working at your desk, for example, consider getting up and moving to another location, in or outside your office, to help you focus on the speaker. Instruct others to not interrupt your time with this person, if necessary. Doing these things may drastically improve how the other person communicates to you.

② Ask this person questions about his or her thoughts and feelings.

Use open-ended questions to draw out new information and clarify what you are hearing. This is especially important when you are trying to understand a relatively taciturn individual who keeps a lot inside. Open-ended questions invite the speaker to expand or elaborate on his or her message. They offer the person more leeway to respond and share. *"What was the upsetting part for you about what he said?" "How do you foresee things getting better on this project?" "Why do you think Bob was so quiet at the meeting?"* Use open-ended questions to encourage others to "open up" and share thoughts, feelings, and opinions. By doing so, you increase your chances of learning what's really important to them. Moreover, the person may respond favorably to your attention and interest.

There are many ways to do this, such as stating or asking

- ❑ *"I'm not sure I know what your thoughts are about . . ."*
- ❑ *"Tell me more about this."*
- ❑ *"What were your reactions/thoughts about . . . ?"*
- ❑ *"Can you give me an example or two?"*
- ❑ *"How come? Why do you feel that way?"*
- ❑ *"I've never asked you about . . ."*

③ Consult other people who may have insights about this person.

Who seems to have more success with this person? Ask for his or her perspective about your challenger and for suggestions on new approaches to try. Even if you find that everyone you know has the same feelings about this person as you do, they may have different ways of coping. You might approach a colleague and say, "I've been really frustrated by _____. What works for you in dealing with him (her)?" The person you are consulting may have some knowledge you lack or a terrific suggestion about how to deal with this challenging individual. If none is forthcoming, at least there are now two of you putting your heads together about this person rather than you tackling the situation all by yourself.

Imagine that you *are* the other person and ask yourself how a specific situation would look to you, what you'd be feeling and what your concerns might be. This is not an easy task. It's hard to put aside your own perspective on the situation.

One suggestion is to appreciate that the other person may look at things differently than you do. For example, you might see the assignments you get as an opportunity to show others how capable you are. The other person might view assignments as simply a job to be done. Although we each have our own preferences and style, it's important to recognize that different doesn't necessarily mean better (or worse). Are right-handed people "better" than lefties?

Here are some ways in which the other person may be different from you:

Spontaneous	⇨ ⇨ ⇨ ⇨ ⇨ ⇨ ⇨	Careful
Social	⇨ ⇨ ⇨ ⇨ ⇨ ⇨ ⇨	Private
Emotional	⇨ ⇨ ⇨ ⇨ ⇨ ⇨ ⇨	Analytic
"Take charge"	⇨ ⇨ ⇨ ⇨ ⇨ ⇨ ⇨	Responsive
Competitive	⇨ ⇨ ⇨ ⇨ ⇨ ⇨ ⇨	Collaborative
Give opinions	⇨ ⇨ ⇨ ⇨ ⇨ ⇨ ⇨	Ask questions
Intense	⇨ ⇨ ⇨ ⇨ ⇨ ⇨ ⇨	Easygoing
Focused	⇨ ⇨ ⇨ ⇨ ⇨ ⇨ ⇨	Multitasking
Confronting	⇨ ⇨ ⇨ ⇨ ⇨ ⇨ ⇨	Avoiding
Self-oriented	⇨ ⇨ ⇨ ⇨ ⇨ ⇨ ⇨	Group-oriented
Respect for talent	⇨ ⇨ ⇨ ⇨ ⇨ ⇨ ⇨	Respect for authority
Loose	⇨ ⇨ ⇨ ⇨ ⇨ ⇨ ⇨	Rule-oriented

Reflecting on how the other person's style may contrast to your own will help you appreciate "their shoes." Notice, for example, that the opposite end of the continuum from "spontaneous" is "careful," not "rigid." A person like Helen, the accountant, someone who is less freewheeling and more deliberate than you, may have a unique contribution to make.

Identify how you typically "dance" with this person. Are you avoiding? Critical? Forgiving? Demanding? Be curious enough to see what would happen if you acted dramatically different. For example, you might consider one of the following new behaviors:

❑ Take extra time to build rapport and establish trust with this person.

❑ Be firmer and more consistent about what you expect from this person.

❑ Take a positive approach by reinforcing and encouraging this person.

❑ Ask this person to tell you about his or her views, needs, and concerns.

❑ Back off on a big change; focus on little ones.

❑ Be more honest and straight with this person about what you think and feel.

❑ Be more persistent with your efforts to influence this person. Don't let up.

 Coaching Contract

Think of someone you find challenging. Ask yourself, "Which of the five steps could I take to understand that person better?"

Looking at Challenging People as Anxious People

We realize that getting the energy to act on these five ways to understand others better can be a tall order. You may be so frustrated, angry, or pessimistic at this point in the relationship that it would require from you an awful lot of resolve to refocus.

One of the best ways to develop anew the energy to be "curious rather than furious" is to consider that all human beings, the challenging as well as the pleasant, have three basic human needs:

- ❑ *Control* is the need to have power over one's life, to be in the driver's seat instead of the passenger seat.
- ❑ *Connection* is the need for belonging, support, love, and acceptance.
- ❑ *Competence* is the need for success, for demonstrating mastery and being recognized for doing so.

At any given time, we may be anxious about obtaining one or more of these needs. To lessen the anxiety, we might go to one of two extremes: excessively pursue the fulfillment of the need or avoid situations in which the need arises. For example, someone who is anxious about *control* might act like a "control freak," who needs everything done his or her way. In contrast, someone who is anxious about being in *control* may decide to let others call the shots. Someone anxious about *connection* might act like a social leech while someone else might withdraw or reject others. Someone anxious about *competence* might be a braggart while someone else might act like a failure.

Imagine you have a co-worker named Steve. Here is how you see him, if you look at him only with fury rather than with curiosity:

Steve is arrogant, opinionated, and sloppy about his work and yet highly critical of others. He often makes crude or insensitive comments to people and reacts very defensively to any type of suggestion or criticism, no matter how constructive.

Steve "stumbled" onto his job at our company, and the job is a little out of his league. He knows it. Yet he won't ask for help or advice.

How might you apply the 3 C's (*control, connection,* and *competence*) to Steve in order to better understand his behavior?

Perhaps Steve is using his arrogance to push people away and avoid connection because he's afraid others will reject him. (And is it just possible that the culture at this company is not as accepting as it could be?) Or Steve may be very insecure about his competence and thinks that he's safer if he keeps people at a distance (and when a mistake leads people to conclude that you're "out of your league," can you blame him?). If we can understand Steve's anxieties, we may be able to relate to him better. For instance, maybe it would be better to connect with him, especially when he's not being obnoxious, and perhaps he'll feel more accepted and less likely to push people away. Maybe if his co-workers complimented his occasional successes, he might be more open to their criticism.

When you think about the people whom you find challenging, consider what may be making them anxious and use that insight to look at them differently and perhaps act toward them differently.

When someone is anxious about control, you might

❑ Keep him or her informed and up to date.

❑ Offer choices and decisions.

❑ Seek agreement ("I thought I'd do x. Is that okay with you?").

❑ Ask, "What role would you like to have in this project?"

When someone is anxious about connection, you might

❑ Make a point of showing the person attention when it's convenient for you.

❑ Tactfully and directly set limits when she or he wants too much of your time.

❑ Offer greetings or conversation in low-keyed, small doses.

❑ Ask a question you know she or he can answer "yes" to.

When someone is anxious about competence, you might

❑ Give genuine positive feedback when you can.

❑ Avoid putting the person on the spot in front of others.

❑ Give the person a task you know she or he can do success-fully.

❑ Praise accomplishments matter-of-factly rather than effusively.

Now that we've offered you some general advice, let's look at some specific situations where the strategy of "being curious rather than furious" will pay off.

Breaking In a New Boss

Q:

"My new boss acts like he knows more than I do about producing our product, even though this is his first year with the company. He doesn't show respect for my knowledge and competence. How am I going to work with him?"

Coaching Tip

Approach a challenging person as if you were an anthropologist.

A: When we don't like or don't understand someone, we have a tendency to write off that person and declare him or her a lost cause. Dismissing or labeling the person may give us a momentary sense of satisfaction, but it doesn't shed any light on the person's behavior. The people-smart alternative is to make a serious effort to understand the person's motives and perspective. This is not the same as liking or accepting the person; it's more like approaching him or her scientifically.

Once you've made the crucial decision to try to understand your boss, there are numerous ways to go about it. One is to ask him questions. That doesn't mean give him the third degree, but rather, interview him in a friendly way to learn more about his views and experiences. You might ask him how he's doing at getting used to the place, what he studied in college, where he's from, and so on. Listen attentively and responsively. You can also give some thought as to how differences between you may be hindering understanding. Differences in style, age, sex, and culture, for example, can sometimes lead to misunderstanding and conflicting viewpoints. If your boss is a young guy who grew up in the age of instant technology (whereas you didn't), perhaps the two of you have different expectations about how long it takes to learn something new.

You can also try to look below the surface and ask yourself what your boss might be anxious about. We all need the 3 C's: control, connection with others, and competence. But sometimes people are overly anxious about one or more of these issues. As the "new kid on the block," your boss may be anxious about whether people more senior than he see him as a competent, capable manager. People who are anxious about competence are very sensitive about appearing uninformed or out of their league in any way. Asking your advice may simply be too threatening a step for your boss to take right now. If you try to help put him at ease and acknowledge his strengths, he may become more open to you in time.

When a Customer Is Furious

Q:

"I hate it when customers unload on me. Whether they have a reason or not, people shouldn't just yell, complain, and carry on. Sometimes it's almost impossible to get a word in edgewise, and I feel like I'm getting ready to blow up, myself. How should I handle these unpleasant situations?"

 Coaching Tip

There's a kernel of truth behind even the most outlandish complaint.

A: When a customer unloads, our instinct is often to strike back (*"Fine, Mr. Norton, then remove your own gall bladder!"*). Alas, this is not the people-smart approach.

Instead, try these three key steps to pacify an angry customer: keep calm, identify the problem, and defuse the anger.

Keep calm. Although it's easier said than done, the first rule in dealing with an irate customer is not to take their anger personally. Do not become defensive. It will only make him or her angrier. You are the company in the customer's eyes, so try to personify the company and give it a compassionate, human voice. It may also help to recognize the customer as someone who is under a lot of stress at the moment. No one is at his or her best under those circumstances. By recognizing the customer as anxious and distressed, it will become a little easier not to take the anger personally.

Identify the problem. Listen. Offer empathy and acknowledgment by succinctly paraphrasing or summarizing what the customer says and by identifying how he or she must be feeling. Ask questions to elicit further information and to clarify the customer's concerns. Find the kernel of truth behind the complaint.

Defuse the anger. Show understanding and acknowledge the customer's point. It's crucial to disarm the customer's anger in this way before you go on to offer a solution, or he or she may not feel heard. When the customer says, *"This rental car is a total mess!"* you might say, *"Yes, used cigarette butts in the ashtray can be really gross. I'm sorry. That shouldn't have gotten by."* If the customer is venting without making a specific request, then after acknowledging their anger, you might reframe by asking, *"What would be a solution to this situation for you?"*

It's always tempting to meet anger with anger, but it's almost never productive to do so. If you can be curious when the customer is furious, the likelihood is that the customer will still be around long after his or her anger is gone.

When You Become the Boss of Former Colleagues

Q: *"I was recently promoted and now supervise several individuals who were my peers within the department. Most of them have accepted the change and treat me with friendly respect. One of them, however, seems to constantly test the limits of our new work relationship. She teases me about being the big cheese, even in front of others, and she pops into my office to pump me for information about what's "really" going on in the organization. Not only that, but she even offers me all sorts of unwanted advice about how to handle others in the department. We had a pretty close relationship, but her behavior is making me want to avoid her now. Is there a tactful way to set her straight?"*

Coaching Tip

As a boss, you may need boundaries more than buddies. Don't be afraid to draw them.

A: You might begin by giving some thought to what may be driving her behavior. Do you think she's afraid of losing her personal connection with you? Or is it more likely that she sees you as a shortcut to the fast lane? By trying to walk in her shoes and identify her motives, you may be better able to decide on the appropriate blend of reassurance and limit setting you can use to redirect her.

Certainly, limits are in order. Tell her calmly but firmly, *"I don't have time to talk right now"* or *"I don't have any news I can share with you"* when she invades your space or pumps you for inside information.

The most effective step you can take is to meet with her and provide some frank feedback about how her behavior is affecting you, along with a specific request for change. You can honor the peer relationship the two of you have had by taking her into your confidence—but on your terms. Tell her something like this:

> *"You know that I value your friendship and I believe I can be completely honest with you. This promotion has put me in a new role and I need some time and space to settle into it. I know you have lots of ideas and enthusiasm, but I'm going to request that you do something important for me. I'd like you to back off a bit for the next three months while I get my feet under my desk and learn my new territory. Please keep sharing your ideas in meetings and when I ask you for suggestions, which I definitely will. But it would help me a lot if you'd give me some leeway right now and let me be the one to come to you. Can you do that for me?"*

It's unlikely she'll refuse such a graciously worded request. Thank her for her help and tell her you know you can count on her. By the time your three-month "grace" period has passed, she'll have adjusted to the change in your relationship. Or else one or both of you will have gotten promoted out of the situation.

Understanding Your Boss's Priorities

Q: "My boss treats my 'in box' like his personal recycling bin. He turns over all kinds of projects to me with no clear indication of what his priorities are. I don't like to keep bugging him with questions, but I need some kind of guidelines about what he expects. Also, some of these assignments are pretty boring and I'd like him to give me more interesting and challenging projects to work on. But I don't know what's important to him."

 Coaching Tip

Walk in your boss's moccasins—and keep a roadmap to remember the route.

A: Trying to grab your supervisor's attention when he's on the run is not a good way to seek his input about priorities. Instead, propose a meeting to discuss the issue and couch your request in terms of wanting to get a better handle on his current goals and concerns so that you can better organize your efforts to support him. Bring your "to do" list to the meeting.

There are various frameworks for assigning priority to tasks. One helpful approach is to consider three dimensions of any task. A project that scores high on all three is the one to start with. See if you and your boss can use this framework as a common language to discuss his goals and concerns.

Urgency. Determine how much external pressure there is to complete the task. Supervisors and customers are major sources of pressure to get things done. Deadlines create urgency as well. You need to understand how your boss perceives the urgency of the tasks he is delegating to you.

Doability. If a task is relatively easy to do and the necessary resources and support are available, it is likely to be accomplished quickly and successfully. You may be in a better position than your boss to assess the doability of a task he assigns you. If doability is low, it's helpful to spell out what it will take to do the job and how this may impact other projects.

Motivation. Here's where your interests come into play. You want more opportunity to work on projects that challenge you. But you need to know more about your supervisor's wish list in order to link your interests to his.

When you meet with your boss, rather than starting with your task list, ask him questions about his current goals, concerns, hopes, and interests. See if you can interpret back to him where the items on your task list fit in. Your aim is to be able to think about assignments the way he does. You might reflect back: *"It sounds like x, y, and z are probably the top priorities right now. I'll get right on them. If I can clear some time by the end of the week, are there any special projects I could start on to help you prepare for your meeting with Briggs next month?"* If you can think of something you'd like to do that would mesh with his needs, suggest it.

Responding to a Critical Co-worker

Q:

"One of my teammates constantly belittles my ideas. He even makes faces and wisecracks during meetings when I speak. I feel like throwing a cup of coffee at him! Why would he treat me this way?"

 Coaching Tip

When someone is getting to you, get a handle on them.

A: Snipers like your co-worker try to elevate themselves at the expense of others. Behavior like this can be infuriating and really tests your ability to work people-smart. But try to get curious enough to answer your own question: Why does he do this? Are you a threat to him? Is he so insecure in his position that he's going to these lengths to look important? Does he crave attention? Use your insights to head him off at the pass.

If you can stand it, try reaching out to him in a proactive way. Share your ideas with him ahead of time and ask for his feedback. Find something you like or respect about him (even if it's just his taste in ties) and comment about it to others. Give this approach a few weeks. You may find that he now derives more self-esteem from being your ally than being your critic.

If this doesn't work, focus on how you respond to his stealth attacks, especially when others are present. When he makes a face or a negative comment, stop your presentation. Just look at him for a long moment, then calmly ask him to share his specific concerns. Stay focused on content and don't refer to how childish his shenanigans are. Try saying something like *"Jim, you seem uncomfortable with this. Please tell me what your reservations are."* If he resists, press him: *"No, please, I'd really like to hear your thoughts."* When he does share, invite others to react. They may become your allies. Depending on the situation, you may also want to acknowledge his implied criticism, but insist on finishing what you have to say *("Jim, I can see you have some issues. If you'll hold your thoughts for another ten minutes, we'll have some time for discussion when I finish the presentation.")*. The principle here is that the sniper is most comfortable shooting from the sidelines, wearing his camouflage gear. By shining a floodlight on him, you expose his game and take control of the situation.

When Someone's Performance Is Slipping

Q:

"One of my direct reports seems to be on the skids. He's normally a good worker, but lately his reports are just not up to par. When I tried to discuss it with him and offer some suggestions for improvement, he got really defensive. I feel like I'm in a bind. I don't see how I can just ignore what's going on, but I don't want to pry or get inappropriately personal either. What's the best way to help this guy?"

Coaching Tip

Don't rush to solve a problem before you understand it.

A: A doctor wouldn't treat symptoms without making a diagnosis. A good mechanic wouldn't try to fix your car without figuring out what's broken. Before you can resolve whatever problem is going on with your direct report, you need to understand it. We suggest you "interview" rather than interrogate him with the goal of learning how **he** sees the situation.

Interviewing is a form of active listening aimed at uncovering information—without putting the other person on the spot. When you interview, key behaviors include the following:

❑ Ask questions and dig for deeper understanding.
❑ Solicit the other person's viewpoint, while holding back on your own.
❑ Seek clarification and illuminate how the other person is feeling.
❑ Demonstrate understanding of what the person is sharing.

Make some time to sit down with your direct report, and start by stating in a calm, straightforward way that you've noticed that his recent reports aren't up to his usual high standards and you'd like to understand how he sees the situation. You might ask, *"How do you think this report compares with what you usually turn in?"* Once you get the ball rolling, make a point of being receptive and responsive to anything he says. An excellent way to do this is by paraphrasing.

When you paraphrase, you feed back, succinctly and in your own words, the most important elements of the person's message. Paraphrasing gets a bad name because people often do it poorly, either by parroting the same words the person just said or by using some hackneyed formula, like *"so I hear you saying . . ."* In contrast, when you capture and reflect the heart of what someone tells you, you begin to gain the person's trust and encourage her or him to open up further. So the interview with your direct report might sound something like this:

You: *"How do you think this report compares with what you usually turn in?"*

D.R.: *"All right, well, it's a little below par. I'm sorry."*

You: *"So you're not entirely happy with it either. Can you tell me what you think may have contributed to the change?"*

D.R.: *"Well, since Jim was transferred to sales, I'm not getting the same information I used to get. I guess the report suffers for it."*

You: *"You sound frustrated."*

D.R.: *"I am! I don't like doing a second-rate job, but I don't see how I can produce the same quality in the same time with less support."*

You can move to a problem-solving mode after you have adequately explored the situation. Your solutions are more likely to be effective when you understand the problem.

When an Unfamiliar Accent Interferes with Your Understanding

Q: *"One of my clients is Asian and speaks with a pretty heavy accent. Often I just can't understand what she's saying. I find this very embarrassing and, much of the time, I just nod and pretend I do understand. For all I know, she's telling me I'm the premier idiot of the Western world and I'm standing there nodding and smiling. But I just feel so self-conscious about asking her to repeat herself all the time. What can I do?"*

Coaching Tip

Let your differences enhance rather than limit your rapport.

A: We recommend that you change your approach, starting with a new mindset about your situation.

Recognize that denying your difficulty in understanding your client is compounding the problem, rather than solving it. Not only do you feel awkward, but you may be missing or misconstruing important information (maybe she said you should **consult with** the premier idiot of the Western world). Besides, your client undoubtedly realizes you don't understand her and doesn't appreciate being patronized or ignored. So we suggest you resolve to address rather than avoid your communication problem with the client.

Our advice: embrace your differences, rather than deny them. Talk about your communication difficulties, but also express your interest in and appreciation for your client's language and culture. Tell her that her accent is unusual, fascinating, charming, or whatever description rings true for you, and acknowledge that sometimes your provincial American ears have trouble deciphering her words. Say, *"It's important to me to understand you completely. I hope you won't be offended if I ask you to repeat yourself or speak more slowly."*

Moreover, don't be afraid to express your respectful curiosity about her background and culture. Ask where she's from and invite her to tell you about her country of origin (e.g., are business practices different there?). When you have difficulty understanding what she says, you might ask her how she would say the same thing in her native language. No doubt, if you try to repeat it, your accent will be a hundred times worse than hers.

It's okay to acknowledge our differences, as long as we do so respectfully. Sometimes ignoring them is like pretending we don't see the elephant sitting in the living room. It's unrealistic and nonproductive.

When Someone Is a Mystery You'd Rather Not Solve

Q:

"I have a colleague who's a total piece of work. She's a real perfectionist. It takes her forever to get anything done, which makes for big headaches when we have to work on a project together. And of course she's never satisfied with what anyone else produces. She doesn't mesh with the team. For instance, on casual Friday, when everyone wears jeans to work, she comes in wearing one of her prissy little suits. She seems to keep people at a distance. I'm generally a pretty friendly, easygoing person, but she's just too much of a challenge to get along with. Do I really have to make the effort, or can I just try to work around her?"

Understanding does not mean acceptance.

A: It isn't very difficult to work with people we enjoy and identify with. Working people-smart entails finding ways to understand and reach out to those we'd rather avoid. You never have to like this person, or give her your vote as employee of the month. But if you find a way to work with her, you'll probably spend less time feeling aggravated and you will look like a real team player.

Consider your co-worker's needs. She seems pretty anxious about control, as if she feels comfortable only when she's the one carrying the ball. What happens when you try to pull the ball away from someone like that? They just hold on more tightly. If you accept that she has this anxiety (even though you don't share it), it becomes easier to choose an approach that may better meet her needs.

When you work with her on a project, make a point of seeking her input up front about how the end product should look, how much time the project will require, and so forth. Keep her informed about your own progress (not because you need a watchdog, but because her anxiety requires it).

By your description, she is out of sync with the style of the group. Maybe she's anxious about being included and anticipates rejection. It's not your job to become her therapist, but if you are persistent about reaching out in a low-key way (just saying "good morning" or asking how her weekend went), over time she may become a little less distant with you. Eventually, others in the office will be seeking your advice on how to deal with her.

Strategy 2:
Include the Listener Rather than Talk at Him or Her

How often do you see a job listing that says, "The candidate must be an effective communicator"? What does it really mean to be an "effective communicator"? Must you have a gift with words? That would be nice, but the bottom line of effective communication is the ability to be understood.

The Ability to Be Understood

Getting your message out so that it is understandable may seem simple enough, but the fact is that nothing is so simple that it cannot be misunderstood. Our average daily vocabulary includes some 800 words—but those words have 14,000 different meanings!

Here are just a few examples of how words can be confusing:

The dump was so full that it had to refuse more refuse.

He could lead if he would get the lead out.

The soldier decided to desert his dessert in the desert.

The insurance was invalid for the invalid.

After a number of injections, my jaw got number.

To make matters even more complicated, meaning is often contextual and idiosyncratic. For instance, if a vegetarian eats vegetables, what does a humanitarian eat? How can a slim chance and a fat chance be the same, while a wise man and a wise guy are opposites? And why is it that when the stars are out they are visible, but when the lights are out they are invisible?

Or consider this rather innocuous office conversation between Bart and Cynthia:

Bart: *Cynthia, I think you should get in the habit of e-mailing me more often.*

Cynthia: (a little agitated) *Why are you saying that? You don't want to see me face to face?*

Bart: *Oh no! I'm only referring to the faxes you send me about your upgrade needs. I find it easier to handle them when they are e-mailed instead of faxed. Is that all right with you?*

Cynthia: *Sure. I'm glad we got that cleared up. I was feeling a little confused about what you meant.*

Since language itself can be confusing and misleading, we can't afford to compound the problem by talking *at* instead of *with* others.

When we drone on, overload people with details, or turn them into mind readers by leaving out important information, we fail to get our points across and may alienate others in the process.

Today's work world is teeming with communication challenges. As organizations scurry to do more with less, people are increasingly harried and on the run. Technology further drives the trend toward "fast food communication." To get their messages across, people-smart individuals practice the strategy of including their listeners and making them their communication partners.

What does it mean to "include the listener"? It means working to create dialogue—a give-and-take that promotes a meeting of the minds—rather than simply broadcasting messages. The verb "communicate" derives from the same root as the word "common," suggesting that effective communication means creating a shared understanding. Unfortunately, most of us would agree that our day-to-day communication rarely meets this standard.

There are many reasons communication so often becomes a one-way street:

We assume too much. Our own mental picture of what we know, think or believe is so clear to us that we forget that others may not be starting from the same page. It's easy to leave out important information that others need in order to fully grasp what we're saying and follow our flow.

We sell the listener short. Conversely, we may assume others are clueless and fail to build on what they already know. When we do this, we run the risk of sounding patronizing and provoking people to tune us out.

We're in a rush. When time is tight, people often try to cram in information, galloping way ahead of the listener, who has long since given up trying to follow.

We cloud the picture. We give too many details up front and fail to convey the big picture. When a journalist is criticized for "burying the lead," it means he or she failed to get the main point of the story into the opening sentences. Many people do this in their daily communication, missing opportunities to include and inform their listeners.

Communication must be a two-way street. When you include the listener in the conversation, you find out what the listener understands and thinks. You then can build on what he or she has received that's accurate or correct what is inaccurate. If you do all the talking, however, you have to guess how the listener is interpreting or reacting to what you are saying.

Four Coaching Tips for Including the Listener

People-smart communicators know that no matter how complex the topic is, how great the time pressures are, or what the mental state of the listener may be, they need to treat their listeners as communication partners. Here are some of the techniques they use:

① Orient the receiver.

Convey the big picture before launching into details. Bear in mind that the nature of the big picture depends on the situation and may appeal to the listener's emotions in addition to highlighting key facts. For example, if you were about to share some very painful information, the big picture might be "I'm afraid I have some very bad news." If the topic is complicated and boring, on the other hand, the big picture might take the form of a brief "headline," such as "The new marketing plan, although complex, is a daring new approach." Here are three strategies for orienting the receiver:

❑ *Ask a question.* Begin by inquiring what the listener already knows or thinks or feels about the topic. This engages the receiver right from the start and gives you clues about what additional information is important.

❑ *Preview coming attractions.* Give a quick overview of what you plan to tell the listener. Think of the way an anchorperson introduces the headlines for the nightly news before launching into the actual stories. If you are sharing complex information, a great strategy is to break it down into three to five key points. Then you can tell the receiver up front, "Our new marketing plan has three key components."

❑ *Start with the bottom line.* Get the receiver's attention up front by stating how she or he will benefit from listening to what you're about to say: "I'm going to describe a marketing plan that could double sales in your division."

When you want someone's full attention and participation in a task, a more detailed orientation can be helpful. Suppose that, as a manager, you are about to conduct a performance review with Joe, a new employee. Joe is anxious about the review and doesn't really know what to expect. You could help Joe participate in the review process through a brief orientation like this:

"Joe, we're going to spend the next hour or so discussing your work performance over the past year and completing this evaluation form together. [You show Joe the form.] I'd like us to do this collaboratively, so that we share our thinking about how you're doing. Let's start by talking about your strengths and accomplishments, then discuss areas for improvement, then goals for the next year. For each of those areas, I'd like you to share your thoughts first, then I'll add mine. If we have any disagreements, we discuss them in more detail. Does that make sense? Do you have any questions about the process?"

 ## ② Feed information in portions.

Instead of trying to share everything at once, offer information in manageable chunks that the listener can process and respond to. When we flood people with information, they'll rarely remember what we just said. A speaker uses an average of 150 words per minute. That's a lot to think about. What happens after a minute or more of nonstop talk? The listener has given up concentrating on what you're saying and is now hearing (but not truly listening) at the rate of 400–500 words per minute. No wonder people's minds wander in the face of an overly talkative person.

When possible, organize complex information ahead of time, whittling it down to three to five main points. Slow down your delivery to give the listener time to digest what he or she is hearing. In the following dialogue, Randy, a supervisor, is a subject matter expert explaining a complicated topic to Phil, a new employee. Notice how Randy feeds him manageable chunks of information to avoid overwhelming him.

Randy: *I'd like to explain how we do clinical trials with our experimental drugs. After we have found a drug to be safe and effective with animals, we get FDA approval to test it on people. There are three phases of human testing. Did you know that?*

Phil: *No, I didn't. I assumed that all the trials were done with one group of subjects.*

Randy: *Actually, there are different subjects for each phase. In a phase I study, the human subjects are not even patients. They are healthy volunteers.* [Randy pauses a while to let this surprising information sink in.]

Phil: *Why in the world do they do that?*

Randy: *That's because the first study is not designed to find out if the drug is effective. It's simply to find out if it is safe. If a limited amount of the drug will not harm a healthy person in any way, it is given to volunteers who are paid to study how the drug affects the human body. There are exceptions, like chemotherapy agents. They can only be given ethically to willing cancer patients, right from the beginning. So far, so good?*

Phil: *Well, I have more questions about this first phase, but let's move on. Tell me about the other two phases.*

Randy: *Phase II and phase III studies are done with patients who might benefit from the drug. Both studies are designed to find out how effective the drug is.* [Randy pauses again.]

Phil: *So what's the difference between the two?*

Randy: *A phase II study takes about two years and involves 100 to 300 volunteer patients to assess the drug's effectiveness in fighting the disease in question. A phase III study lasts about three years and usually involves 1,000 to 3,000 patients in clinics and hospitals. Physicians monitor patients closely to determine efficacy and identify adverse reactions.*

Make sure you and your receiver are speaking the same language. For example, would your listener be more familiar with "horizontal/vertical" or "landscape/portrait" in describing page orientation? Avoid technical terms or jargon that may be foreign to your listener. Incorporate metaphors that match his or her experience and interests (if you're talking about teamwork with a sports buff, football analogies are great; if the listener is more the artistic type, you might do better to evoke images of a dance ensemble). Don't hesitate to ask the listener whether a word or phrase is unfamiliar. Many people are reluctant to express ignorance and will act as if they understand when they don't.

To illustrate the need to be "listener-friendly," consider the following exchange between a call center manager, seeking training for her employees, and a training director:

Training director: *In order to build an effective instructional design for your employees, we'll need to do a front-end analysis initially to determine the competency set you require.*

Call center manager: *Can you say that again in plain English?*

Training director: *Sorry about that. What I meant is that effective training is built around understanding the skills your employees must have and how well they perform in doing their jobs. For example, let's say that your people must enter brief but accurate records of past conversations with customers into their computers. However, many of them don't handle this part of their job well. In that case, we can study where their performance is subpar and address that specific training need. This becomes part of the "competency set" that the training will deliver. Am I clearer this time?*

Call center manager: *Yes, much better. Now that I understand you, how do we get started with this "front-end analysis"?*

When you communicate, be more of a talk show host than a lecturer. Find ways to bring the listener into the discussion in order to involve him or her and ensure understanding. Here are three ways to do this:

❑ *Respond to nonverbal cues.* If the listener looks confused, stop and explore what's puzzling him or her, rather than going on and on in an effort to make your point. If the receiver seems to be reacting with any strong emotion, positive or negative, reflect this ("You seem surprised." "You look excited.").

❑ *Actively check in with the listener.* Take the "pause that refreshes." See if the receiver has questions or reactions you can build on to make your point. Use such phrases as

    ❑ *So far, so good?*

    ❑ *Before we go further, do you have any questions?*

    ❑ *How am I doing?*

    ❑ *Have I been clear? Helpful?*

    ❑ *What are you thinking at this point?*

❑ *Invite feedback.* Ask the receiver to restate what he or she has heard. You can do this without being patronizing. Say to the listener, "Would you mind giving me a quick recap of what I've told you so I can see if I've been clear?" Or "So what would you say to someone unfamiliar with this topic if you had to explain it?"

Coaching Contract

Select a situation in which you need to communicate information effectively to someone. Which of our tips would you use? How would you apply them?

If these strategies for including the listener seem time-consuming, don't be fooled. Failing to make others into communication partners wastes more time in the long run. This is true even in tense and tricky workplace situations. Notice how our people-smart communication strategies apply in the scenarios that follow.

Making Complicated Assignments Clear

Q:

"We have some pretty detailed safety procedures in our plant, and it's vital that employees understand and follow them. Unfortunately, this doesn't always happen. I've found that I can't rely on subordinates to read procedure manuals, so I try to explain the most important procedures in a face-to-face orientation. But half the time, I can see I'm losing them. Any advice?"

 Coaching Tip

First get their full attention. The details come later.

A: People can record and retain a surprising amount of detailed information under two key conditions:

❑ The information is really important to them.

❑ It's organized in a user-friendly way.

Keeping this in mind, here are some strategies you can use to orient your people to crucial (but somewhat boring) procedures.

Start with the big picture. Sometimes the best way to do this is to ask a powerful question that focuses the other person on the topic, such as "What do you think are some of the ways a person could get seriously injured using this equipment?"

Feed information in manageable chunks. Break a procedure down into no more than three to five steps. Make sure the listener absorbs each one before you move on to the next.

Get visual. If you can demonstrate or show an example of how something is done, it will help get the person's attention.

Check in with the receiver. Allow the person to ask questions, react, and digest what you are saying. Invite him or her to feed back what he or she has heard.

If you use these tips and you still see that you're losing them, stop talking. Acknowledge that they look lost and explore what's happening, instead of going on and on in an effort to make your point. If necessary, refer back to how the employee will benefit from learning the procedure, for instance, by asking, "Do you believe that information can really protect you?" If the answer is no, share a couple of horror stories: "I guess you don't remember poor old Fred . . ."

When the Clock Is Running

Q:

"I'm often expected to give a presentation to my customers or colleagues without adequate time allowed to cover all the important points. When this happens, I feel like a deer caught in the headlights. I either freeze up or go to the other extreme and talk too fast, trying to get everything in. Obviously, neither approach works. Any solutions?"

Coaching Tip

Better to leave them hungry for more than overstuffed.

A: Stop trying to do the impossible. Pretending you can walk on water just leaves you with wet feet. A presentation is not a final exam in which you must show mastery of the whole semester's content. Rather, your goal should be to capture your listeners' interest so that they are prepared to give you more of their time and attention later.

Instead of attempting to cover everything, choose one or two key points you want to make and make them in the most compelling way you can. Remember that your audience will be more attentive when you involve them, rather than talk at them. Don't be afraid to invite questions and discussion, right up front. Good trainers try to integrate "tell, show, do" elements into their presentations because they know that demonstrations and hands-on practice opportunities promote learning better than lectures alone. So look for ways to invite people's active participation, even in brief presentations.

When you really need to impart more information (say, because the customer demands it even though time is limited), let your handouts do some of the talking. You can supply more detailed information in the form of materials your customers can study at their leisure. Instead of trying to review all of the contents in your talk, just orient your customers to the materials. They don't need you to read it to them.

When Someone Doesn't Speak the Group Language

Q:

"Most of the people on my project team are guys and they talk 'guy language'—sports, cars, and so forth. Sometimes I can see the women just rolling their eyes, and I guess they feel kind of left out of the discussion. As the team leader, is there something I should do to bring them in?"

Coaching Tip

Being on the same team doesn't automatically mean being on the same page.

A: There are many situations where "group speak" tends to exclude some members of a team. Gender metaphors are just one example. Women may be more comfortable using feeling words; men may be more apt to interrupt. Cultures have different norms about speaking up and expressing opinions. In addition, almost every industry, or even every company, has its own jargon that can be confusing to outsiders and newcomers. Most of the time, these "languages" are so established in the group culture that people aren't even aware that they are using them, leaving the odd person out to suffer in silence.

As a team leader or concerned colleague, what can you do to help include the outsiders? Here are some suggestions:

Seek out newcomers and offer to "translate." Acknowledge that some terms may be unfamiliar and normalize any confusion they may be feeling. Offer to explain words or expressions that are unclear ("Sean, you looked confused when Sandy referred to the 'lunch and learn' program. Would it help if I explained . . . ?"). If new hires typically receive procedure manuals or other orientation materials, consider incorporating a glossary of common "inside" terms.

Incorporate minority language. Notice metaphors or phrases that individuals tend to use when you talk with them individually, and find opportunities to bring them into the group discourse ("Malti was talking about masala the other day, and it struck me that an effective team can also be a blend of spices . . .").

Vary metaphors. Instead of relying on the usual expressions, surprise people with a new image once in a while, perhaps one that might be more mainstream. If the guys usually describe a team player by saying, "He knows when to lay down a bunt, instead of trying to hit it out of the park every time," try offering up an alternative like "You folks managed that project like an ensemble cast in a hit show!"

Language is one of the most powerful tools we have for including or excluding others. It's people-smart to notice when a work group uses language divisively and to take the initiative to invite outsiders in.

When You Owe an Apology

Q:

"I committed a major blunder with a customer. Don't ask for the details; it's too humiliating to say. But my error makes me look foolish and will hurt the client where he's most vulnerable: in his wallet. Obviously, I must apologize, but how?"

Coaching Tip

To err is human; to apologize well is essential.

A:

Your question is understandable, since there are so many examples of wretched apologies out there today. When public figures make pseudo apologies like "If my words inadvertently caused offense to anyone, then I regret it," we all roll our eyes and think, *"The idiot doesn't get it."* This is exactly the kind of message you don't want to deliver to your seething customer. If any situation calls for including the listener, it's the offering of an apology.

It *is* possible to deliver a sincere and gracious apology. Besides being good for the soul, it can be helpful to the situation. In quality improvement, a business disaster becomes an opportunity to demonstrate to the customer your concern, good faith, and resourcefulness. So let's look at how to express an apology that your customer will actually hear and appreciate.

There are five R's that go into an effective apology: **responsibility, recognition, reason, regret, and reparation.**

Responsibility. Acknowledge your mistake and admit it was your fault. Don't be vague about what the mistake was. Identifying exactly what you did wrong shows that you're sincerely accepting culpability ("I know I was supposed to purchase those shares for you yesterday, Mr. Trump. The truth is, I forgot to place the order.").

Recognition. Show that you understand the impact of your mistake. Describe, from the customer's frame of reference, the most important tangible and emotional costs of your error ("I realize my mistake has cost you a potentially lucrative business opportunity and seriously damaged your trust in me.").

Reason. People often want to know why your mistake happened, but they will be turned off if they perceive you as making excuses. To err is human; to take yourself off the hook or blame others is dumb ("My wife is scheduled for some surgery, and I allowed it to distract me. I should have realized I wasn't operating at full speed and taken some personal time.").

Regret. Share your regret as sincerely and eloquently as you can ("I'm so sorry to have let you down like this.").

Reparation. If you can identify anything you might do to offset or compensate for the damages to the customer, offer to do so. You might also ask the customer to suggest a way for you to make recompense ("Mr. Trump, I'll certainly understand if you want to switch to a new account exec. But before you do, perhaps you'll allow me to represent you without taking any commission for the next three months.").

Although there's no guarantee that your apology will turn the tide, remember that "to forgive is divine." Your customer may derive a sliver of self-esteem from magnanimously forgiving you. If not, at least you may take a step toward forgiving yourself.

When You Don't Believe They "Get It"

Q:

"I explained a new project to my assistant yesterday. When I asked her if she had any questions, she said no, and when I asked her if she understood her role in the project, she nodded. But I just don't think she really got it. Is there a way to make sure someone understands instructions without making them look stupid?"

Coaching Tip

Sometimes a simple question results in a too-simple answer.

Don't ask, "Do you understand?" or "Is that clear?" Direct questions like these require only a simple yes/no answer, which tells you next to nothing. Your assistant may *think* she or he understands your instructions and prove otherwise after the damage is already done.

Here are three alternative approaches you can use to check out someone's understanding of your instructions.

Request an instant playback. Invite the other person to feed back, in his or her own words, what he or she understood you to say. The challenge is to do this in a way that the other person won't find patronizing. Instead of saying, "Now, what did I ask you to do?" try "I've hit you with a lot of new information, and I want to make sure I haven't confused you. Would you please take a moment and sum up what you think I'm asking of you?"

Ask "what if . . . ?" Toss a few "curve balls," or hypothetical scenarios, to the other person to see if they can apply your instructions. Again, do this in a way that won't seem insulting. Tell your assistant, "These instructions may sound pretty straightforward, but sometimes they may be hard to interpret. For instance, what would you do if . . . ?"

Say "show me." Invite your assistant to give you a brief demonstration of the behaviors or tasks you've outlined, presenting it as a rehearsal that will allow you both to test out the procedure (not the person). Alternatively, suggest a trial run or pilot period so that both of you can evaluate the procedure and modify it as needed.

When Your Boss Has No Time to Listen

Q:

"My boss is stretched so thin that a few minutes of her time are a precious commodity. When I do get a chance to speak with her, I feel really pressured because I need to update her on the status of my projects and get her input on areas where I'm unclear. Not only do I fail to get through my agenda, I often can't even get to my highest-priority items. How can I make the most of the time she allots me?"

 Coaching Tip

With a busy boss, think: "Lights, Camera, Action!"

A: Under this type of pressure it's easy to fall into the trap of trying to cover too much and ending up communicating too little. We suggest you take as your template the anchor on the nightly newscast. Think about how much ground this person covers in just a few minutes and see if you can adapt some of his or her strategies. Here are some approaches you might consider.

Determine your time slot. Try to get clear with your boss in advance how much time she can give you. Confirm this at the outset of the meeting ("So, Jennifer, we have twenty minutes this afternoon, right?"). Monitor the clock discreetly and be prepared to say something like "I see we have about five minutes left and I'd like to make sure we touch on . . ."

Be prepared. Does Tom Brokaw stand up there and free-associate? Plan out not just your agenda, but a bit of a script. Prepare a few key talking points that get to the heart of the issues. Whenever possible, send your boss a memo ahead of time to share some of the details so you can focus on the big picture, the key decisions, and so forth.

Establish the lead stories. Try to get the priorities clear at the outset. The newscast begins with the headlines and saves the human interest stuff for the last few minutes. Tell your boss, "I've got six agenda items and the two that are most important to me are . . ." Again, if you have sent your boss a brief advance memo, she should know what your agenda is. If her priorities are different from yours, it helps to clarify this sooner rather than later.

Interview your boss. It won't do any good to try to cover material if she isn't really listening. Try to ask powerful, focused questions that elicit her most valuable input: "What's your biggest concern about this project?" "What would you say are the major goals here?" "What would you do first if you were me?" If her time is that valuable, treat her like a guest celebrity on your show and share the microphone adroitly. Do this well, and she may be more willing to make return appearances.

Announcing Unpopular Policies

Q:

"I'm a middle manager, with a capital 'Middle.' Our CEO insists we implement some new policies that I know will meet with a lot of resistance from my staff. I don't even agree with the policies myself, but I really have no choice. How can I present these changes to my staff?"

 Coaching Tip

Sometimes you must help your people accept and cope with bad news.

A: Ever since Moses came down from the mountain, leaders have had to enforce commandments from above. When those commandments are unpopular–or even stupid–the task is a difficult one. Here are some dos and don'ts to bear in mind.

Don't make it sound better (or worse) than it is. Avoid sugar-coating the bad news. Your staff will learn the truth anyway, and their trust in you will be diminished. On the other hand, don't present the changes as something terrible. When people expect a catastrophe, they usually find one.

Don't offer false hope. If your staff are hoping the changes won't really happen, or won't apply to them, correct their mistaken impressions. You need to be the voice of reality.

Don't join the resistance. Although you don't have to pretend to like the changes, avoid bad-mouthing the CEO or his or her decisions. Don't suggest or support any proposal to sidestep or sabotage the new policies. To do so would be to court dangerous consequences for yourself and your staff.

Do present the policy in a straightforward way. Describe the changes in neutral, descriptive terms. Clarify how the policy will affect your people. If the CEO has given a rationale for the changes, share it (unless you've been specifically told not to do so).

Do acknowledge their concerns and feelings. Allow some venting, but not prolonged complaining. Show empathy and sum up the group's major reactions and concerns so that they feel heard and validated. It can help to point out that people often feel anxious or angry when facing change.

Making an Effective Presentation

Q:

"Whenever I have to give a presentation to my clients or colleagues, I become a nervous wreck. I guess it's stage fright. My heart pounds, my hands sweat, and I'm always afraid I'll blow it. How can I control my anxiety and be effective as a presenter?"

Coaching Tip

Once you break the ice, the water is usually fine.

A: Performance anxiety generally decreases with practice, so don't give up. Research shows that most nervous speakers overrate how apparent their anxiety is to others, so odds are you look and sound better than you feel.

Most performance anxiety stems from negative assumptions people make about how others will perceive them. If you can make more positive, realistic statements to yourself about how people will receive your message, it will help you relax. Since you are the one giving the presentation, you are probably the person who is most knowledgeable about your topic. Remind yourself of that, by saying to yourself, *"If not you, who?"*

Next, make small talk with early arrivals. It will help you see them as people, rather than as "The Audience." When you give the actual presentation, try to breathe normally, stand up straight, and make eye contact with your clients or colleagues. Smile. Using humor is fine, but don't feel you have to come up with snappy one-liners. Often, the best way to open your presentation is with a question that elicits your listeners' preexisting knowledge or attitudes about your product. This not only helps tune you in to their perspective, but may establish a dialogue that puts everybody at ease.

Remember that most performance anxiety decreases after the first few minutes of a presentation. If you focus on getting off to a good start, you'll probably find the rest of the presentation to be relatively smooth sailing. If your anxiety persists or recurs, you might try interpreting it as a signal to reconnect with your participants. Try opening the floor for questions or inviting their feedback about what you've shared so far.

When People Tune You Out

Q:

"I know I'm not a great communicator. A couple of trusted colleagues have told me, in a nice way, that I tend to drone on, both in meetings and in one-on-one conversations. And I do see people's attention wander when I'm talking. I'm never going to be Mr. Excitement, but I'd like to do a better job of holding people's interest. What are some realistic steps I can take?"

 Coaching Tip

He who lectures is lost.

A: It's easy to fall into the habit of being a "lazy" communicator, just trying to get the words out instead of really putting yourself in the listener's shoes. The truth is that we *earn* people's attention by considering their needs when we talk with them. Here are three steps you can take to make others your communication partners.

Speak in paragraphs, not pages. Try to make your points in brief, compelling statements. When people communicate in writing, it often turns out that the last lines of their piece should have been their opening statement. Try to identify your key message and get right to it. Then pause to let people respond. If this doesn't come naturally to you, try counting to 5 before you start to speak again.

Watch people's reactions. Get in the habit of looking at your listeners and noticing their expressions and body language. Are they making eye contact with you, nodding or otherwise indicating they're following you? If you see them looking away, fidgeting, or worse, yawning, take this as a warning signal and change your approach. Remember, it doesn't matter whether they're tuning you out because you are boring or because they are distractible. The end result is the same: They're not with you.

Invite the listener in. When you detect people tuning out, encourage them to take a more active role. Ask for their reactions in creative ways. Instead of the proverbial "Any questions?" try "Which parts of what I've said so far are unclear?" or "Please share your reactions with me." If people look bored, you might say, "Maybe I'm going too slowly here. Would it help if I pick up the pace?" Use questions throughout your delivery to keep others involved. Try to engage listeners in thinking along with you instead of passively receiving your words.

Strategy 3:

Speak up (with Tact) Rather than Suffer in Silence

Many organizations are not places where you can speak freely. There are several reasons for this. Consider the following:

- ❑ When you speak frankly to someone in your personal life, there's a good chance what you say goes no further than the two of you. In organizations, what one person says is often passed along to others. Unless you've requested that something you say be held in confidence, sooner or later it will be mentioned to a third party and then the whole office knows. With this in mind, most people censor what they really think and feel.

- ❑ For an organization's culture to work, there has to be an adequate amount of agreement and conformity. The positive term for this is "organizational alignment." Sometimes, however, things go too far. People are afraid to disagree with or object to the party line.

- ❑ Today's organizations depend on teamwork and collaboration. Unfortunately, sometimes when individuals speak up, they are accused of not being "team players" when, in fact, they are simply moving beyond the narrow role of "people pleasers."

What happens when you and others in your organization fail to speak up? You suffer in silence, and others are not privy to your feelings and needs. You seethe inside and feel less positive about your job. Others are denied your input. You lose and they lose.

Of course, you don't need to express everything that's on your mind. The key consideration is how important the matter is to your ability to serve the organization effectively. You are not very helpful to the common cause if you

- ❑ Fail to convey your misgivings about how a project is going
- ❑ Agree to goals and objectives you really don't support
- ❑ Allow others to make requests of your time and energy that impede your job performance
- ❑ Brood over your lack of importance to others
- ❑ Excuse behavior that should not be tolerated

How, then, do you go about the sensitive task of speaking up so that you and others benefit? The first challenge is to communicate honestly without being hurtful or putting others on the defensive. Here are some suggestions.

Stand Behind What You Say

Make "I" statements when you want to share your feelings or views. If what you mean is "I don't think we are getting at the core problem of why sales are down," don't say, "Don't you think there are other factors at work here?" If you are not sure you have been understood, don't say, "Do you understand?" Say instead, "Am I making sense?"

Everyone is entitled to a perspective. You don't have to air all of your views all of the time, but when you choose to share what's on your mind, accept the fact that it is *your* opinion, not the absolute truth. Say, " I think this plan is misguided," rather than "This plan is misguided." Or "I'm not feeling I have enough latitude in this matter," rather than "You're micro-managing!"

At the same time, avoid qualifying what you think and feel by using phrases such as "kind of," "sort of," "maybe," "really," and "a little" as you make your point. Don't hedge so much. Be clear:

- ❏ *"I'm angry."*
- ❏ *"I disagree."*
- ❏ *"I don't believe you."*
- ❏ *"I admire you."*
- ❏ *"You're correct."*

Focus on the Problem, Not the Person

Talking straight doesn't mean you have to make others defensive. People get uptight when their control is removed or when their self-esteem is under attack. When you speak up, use clear, descriptive language. Avoid words such as "always" and "never"—even if you are complimenting someone. It's a no-brainer that it's infuriating to say to someone, "You never say anything nice." But think about the impact of saying to someone, "You always do a great job!" You might be implying that the person better not have a "bad day."

If you can describe someone's behavior—without interpreting it—you will be far more likely to address the problem without offending the person. Better to say, "You are not letting me finish" than "You don't care what I have to say, do you?!" In addition, don't control the solution by saying something like "We must stay within our budget," when you could share the problem by saying, "I'm worried that we are over budget. What can we do about it?"

Let's apply this advice to an everyday situation at work. Imagine that you have been upset about an overly friendly co-worker (a "schmoozer") who hangs around you a lot, chatting about matters that are not work related, and doesn't give you enough privacy or time to get your work done. Sometimes you try to get rid of the schmoozer with some excuse, but he doesn't pick up on your hints. You realize that the time has come to address the problem. How might you deal with this situation?

You might continue hinting with words like "Boy, is it 11 o'-clock already?" Or you might try to gamely continue working in his presence, giving him just the slightest attention until he picks up the hint. Or, in frustration, you might try a little veiled ridicule or embarrassment with words like " Don't you ever have work to do?" Instead, consider a more straightforward approach. Concentrate on what you are experiencing because of his schmoozing: "I have a problem. When you come to visit me, I enjoy our conversations, but I get behind in my work. It would help me if we could 'shoot the breeze' over lunch instead."

It's hard enough to speak freely about your ideas and feelings. It's even tougher when you are asserting your needs. For example, others may want something from you and you would rather not do it (your boss wants you to undertake an assignment that is not a good use of your talents), or you want something from others that may be an imposition (assistance in completing a project).

Assertiveness Begins Within

Unless you believe in your right to assert your needs and the value to others of your doing so, you won't be effective when you try to do it. It's people-smart to develop your assertiveness skills for many reasons. Here are some benefits that assertive people reap:

People respect individuals who are forthright. When people are straightforward, others generally admire their courage and personal strength.

People adhere to their boundaries and limits. The quiet firmness of assertive people goes a long way toward influencing others to respect their expectations. Because their style does not arouse anger, others are more willing to comply.

They often get what they want without destroying the relationship. Assertive people stand up for themselves but in a manner that does not demean the other person. As a result, the other person accepts the assertive person's limits as a necessary component of their relationship. In contrast, demeaning or avoiding others may jeopardize the relationship.

They have a strong sense of personal power. The more people-smart individuals assert what they need and obtain a positive response, the more confident they become. This enables them to act in an assured manner the next time. Their self-assurance builds on itself.

They are rarely abused by aggressive people. Assertive people don't fall prey to bullies because they are adept at setting limits and protecting themselves. They are clear about their own rights, as well as those of others, and stand their ground with grace and tact.

They have a grip on their emotions under stress. No one is immune to becoming emotional under trying circumstances, but assertive people know how to readjust and relax because they remain focused on their goals and stay on track.

Their calmness helps others to be calm. When you yell at someone, he or she might be inclined to yell back. When you are calm, the other person is inclined to be calm. Even when someone is yelling at you, if your response is calm, then the person starts to bring it down a notch or two. The ability of assertive people to remain calm under fire helps keep everyone calm.

Guidelines for Asserting Your Needs

Before saying a word, you need to be *clear* up front about exactly what you want to accomplish. Let's apply this rule to the following example.

You are feeling overwhelmed because your boss gives you more assignments than you can handle effectively. Before you speak up, consider first what you want to request. Fewer assignments? His priority list? Additional resources? An advance warning? Maybe you want all of these things ideally, but what's your realistic goal here? That's what getting clear is all about.

People also need to know *how insistent you are*. If you think of your level of insistence as being on a 1 to 10 scale, how strongly do you feel about your present need? If you feel that your need is a 10, but you're only making it sound like a 1, the other person doesn't know how important the issue is to you. On the other hand, if you make your needs sound like a 10 all the time, you become like the boy who cried "wolf" and lose credibility. Consider the following example:

You are continually asked to provide computer assistance to those in your department who are not as adept as you. If you basically have no problems with providing this assistance, you might respond to the next request by saying, "Okay, I'll help you out, but I would appreciate it if I could teach you how to do it yourself sometime. How does that sound?" If you are feeling a bit put off by the requests of others, you might say, "I need to let you know that I'm feeling overwhelmed by the requests I've been getting. I'll give you some help when I can, but I will have to say no sometimes and I hope you'll understand." If you feel that the entire situation has gotten out of hand, you might insist: "Sorry, folks. I must say no to your requests for computer assistance. I have all I can handle just to complete what's on my plate. Please ask for help elsewhere."

Once you are clear about where you stand and how insistent you are, you are in a much better position to express yourself

Coaching Contract

Think of a work situation in which you would like to refuse a request that seems unreasonable or speak up for your needs. Exactly what do you want in this situation? On a 1 to 10 scale, how insistent do you want to be? What brief rationale might you give for your refusal or request?

Once you are clear about where you stand and how insistent you are, you are in a much better position to express yourself calmly and confidently. Here are some tips to help you speak up clearly . . . and with tact.

 Take a deep breath and slow yourself down.

If you rush yourself, you're likely to come across as having little confidence. Your body language is key. People pick up subtle cues in your body language that suggest that they can get the upper hand. Tone of voice, gestures, and eye contact greatly affect the way another person decides how insistent you are, no matter how carefully you select your words.

② Use clear, direct statements.

Having clarified what you want, you are now ready to express your need to the other person. Don't beat around the bush. That makes others suspicious and defensive. Go through the front door instead of the back! Use phrases like

❑ *"I would appreciate it if you . . . (call me first thing in the morning)."*

❑ *"I will not . . . (be able to come to the meeting)."*

❑ *"It would be great if you . . . (could give me a day's notice)."*

❑ *"I will have to . . . (turn down your request)."*

❑ *"Please . . . (tell me when you are ready for the next assignment)."*

❑ *"I would prefer that you . . . (get assistance from someone with more free time)."*

❑ *"It works best for me if . . . (you put it in writing)."*

❑ *"I've decided not to . . . (be on the committee)."*

Avoid such questions as "Don't you think you could have informed me first?" Rhetorical appeals almost never get results. To help you avoid them (if the habit is well engrained), *focus on what you want* from the other person whenever he or she is doing something that interferes with your needs. Often, there is a tendency to *comment on the person's behavior* instead.

③ Explain your reasons . . . briefly.

Usually, asserting your needs requires an explanation. The key is to explain yourself so that you are informative without being defensive. Give a brief, respectful, honest explanation for your position, as in "I don't want to work this weekend because I haven't had quality time with my family recently." Too often, people go on and on justifying themselves as if their position is not justifiable until others agree with them (which they seldom do). If you stop rather than go on and on, you allow breathing room for the other person to reply and even to object. Don't be concerned about that. You can't filibuster forever. Allowing room for a response demonstrates your confidence that you can handle whatever happens.

If you find that the other person is not initially responsive to your needs, avoid arguing. Calmly restate what you want, trying to say the same thing in new words.

For example, imagine you asked a colleague to send you a report you need immediately and you didn't get it. Don't say, "Why didn't you get me that report!?" Instead, you might say something like "I thought you agreed to send me that report. It was important to me. Please keep your word. I count on it." If you get objections, use phrases such as

"That may be."

"We see it differently."

"That's true, and . . ."

"I realize how important this is to you, and . . ."

Here is an illustration of how these tips can be followed.

Timothy is getting ready to leave for the evening. Alyssa, his project leader, approaches him about working on the project over the weekend.

Alyssa: *Timothy, I need you to come in to work again this weekend. We have that deadline looming!*

Timothy: *I thought last weekend was the last time. We have worked every weekend for a month. My family will not be happy.*

Alyssa: *Timothy, when you signed on to this project, you said you could work some weekends.*

Timothy: *Alyssa, you're right. I said* some *weekends, not every weekend. Please ask for more time on this project or find additional time during the day. I am not willing to work another weekend.*

Alyssa: (backing off when confronted with Timothy's assertiveness) *Okay, I hear you. I'm glad you spoke up. We'll just have to ask for more time on the project.*

Now that we've taken a brief look at ways to speak up with tact, let's explore some tense situations you may have encountered at work and coach you in how to handle them.

When Your Boss Asks Too Much

Q:

"A combination of business travel and working overtime is causing me to spend so much time away from my family that my kids barely recognize me and my wife hardly speaks to me. How can I get my boss to be more reasonable in her expectations of me?"

 Coaching Tip

When you take a stand, first build a solid platform.

A: When your job consistently stretches into extra hours and miles, the first thing to do is *assess the situation.* Consider whether there is a compelling business rationale for the demands your boss is placing on you, whether others are sharing the load in an equitable way, and whether it was made clear up front that your job would require this much travel and overtime. Based on your assessment, decide on the position you will take with your boss. Do you want to just plant a seed and give her time to rethink her expectations of you? Or are you prepared to insist on a change, even if it means beginning to look for another job?

Based on your assessment, your next step is to *speak up* and state your position calmly and clearly to your boss. Maybe this entails saying no to a specific request ("I'm sorry, Alice, but I just can't work this weekend. It's my daughter's high school graduation and we've made plans. I'll be glad to put in some extra time during the week on this project."). Or perhaps you would prefer to negotiate the general issue of your boss's demands ("Alice, I'd like to discuss the amount of overtime and travel I'm putting in. Perhaps you're not aware of how many hours it's been amounting to recently. I'm seriously concerned that I'm on overload and it's affecting the quality of my work."). In sharing a rationale for your boss to reconsider her demands, you are more likely to be persuasive if your reasons are business related rather than personal. Perhaps you can show your boss that the heavy travel and overtime have negative consequences for other projects or business relationships.

When you negotiate with your boss, try to *suggest alternatives* that will meet her needs. Is it possible to recruit a colleague to share some of the load? Some people like business travel more than others. Are there other projects—even very unpopular ones—that you might volunteer for in lieu of travel or overtime? Could you do some overtime work at home, so that you at least get a little more time with your family?

Although there is no guarantee that your boss will respond favorably to your appeal, it's worth trying. You'll be clearer about where you stand, and your family will appreciate your efforts.

Getting Co-workers to Pull Their Weight

Q:

"It seems like I'm always the one who puts in the extra time and effort when my team has a deadline. Why don't the others ever offer to pitch in and do their fair share?"

Coaching Tip

Don't make people into mind readers.

A: Your co-workers might be willing to pull their weight, but they cannot read your mind. Although the inequity of the situation is obvious to you, it might not be obvious to them. Maybe your colleagues simply don't notice your efforts, or, if they do, perhaps they tell themselves that you prefer to do the work yourself.

If you haven't been up front and clear with your co-workers, it's time to tell them how you feel and what you want from them. First think through your position: Exactly what are you seeking from each of your colleagues? Decide how insistent you're prepared to be, and prepare a brief rationale for your request. Once you're clear on your position, speak up. Stay calm and confident, and don't blow your cool if you encounter resistance. Instead, stand your ground, acknowledge objections, and reiterate what you want: "Doris, I understand that this is a bad week for you. But Frank expects our report on Friday, and it's going to take some overtime by both of us to get it done. Which section will you take?"

Another approach is to sit down with your co-workers and give them some feedback about the way you see your respective contributions (e.g., "Doris, it seems to me that I'm usually the one who volunteers to work late when there's a deadline. I'm willing to do my share, but do you think we could talk about some ways to share the load more equitably?"). Don't wait for a crisis before doing this. Pick a quiet time and calmly share your perspective of the situation, how it affects you and the team's productivity. Offer specific examples and suggestions for improvement. Then note how your co-workers are responding and ask what they would be willing to do to change things.

When You Lose Your Cool with Subordinates

Q:

"I hate to admit this, but once in awhile I just lose it with some of my staff. Last week I yelled at my assistant and called her incompetent after she mixed up some appointments in my schedule. I know I need to find a better way to handle my anger when their behavior gets to me. But how?"

Coaching Tip

Learn to be quick to speak up and slow to blow up.

A: People sometimes think that only the meek need to develop assertiveness skills. But the reality is that aggression misses the mark just as much as passivity does.

And because hostility is more conspicuous than wimping out, it can get you into hot water more quickly. Even when you're the boss, you can't get away with this kind of behavior.

Ironically, many people who tend to blow their tops need to become more adept at expressing their wants, needs, and limits with others. By speaking up calmly and clearly, you can take the guesswork out of communicating your expectations to others, rather than hoping for the best and accumulating resentment. Think through the "fine print" before you give assignments to your direct reports. Spell out the specific "who, what, when, where, and how" details of what you want done, in advance. Invite their questions so you can clarify any misunderstandings up front.

In addition to managing your staff more effectively, you can do a better job at managing your emotional responses. Learn to recognize your personal warning signs of anger building, whether it's clenching your jaw muscles, feeling knots in your stomach, or wanting to throw something. Become aware of the "tapes" you typically play in your head that keep your anger fueled (e.g., thoughts like "she *always* does this" or "mistakes like this will sink the whole project"). When you feel yourself building up steam, change your tape. See if you can think more neutrally about the situation, instead of taking things personally or catastrophizing. Take a few deep breaths, a drink of water, or a walk around the block, and *don't* try to talk with the person who's angered you until you are calm. Try writing a script of what you can say, editing out anything inflammatory before you approach the person. Practice expressing disappointment or dissatisfaction by making "I" rather than "you" statements. "I'm unhappy with this report" sounds better than "You did this wrong."

Be patient with yourself as you work on these issues. Getting angry with yourself doesn't work out any better than getting angry at your staff. If you slip and lose it with someone, apologize and let the person know that you'll try to do better in the future. People will appreciate your efforts.

When a Colleague Makes Unwanted Overtures

Q:

"One of my co-workers has been sending me signals that he's interested in a personal relationship. He finds excuses to talk to me, compliments me about my appearance, and has been dropping hints about going to various weekend events. So far, I've managed to keep my distance, but I'm sure it's just a matter of time before he actually asks for a date. He's a nice enough guy, but I'm just not interested. How do I brush him off without creating a major incident?"

Coaching Tip

Just say no.

A: Fortunately, that little word "no" comes in more flavors than Baskin-Robbins ice cream. Which one you choose to serve in this case depends on how persistent, unwelcome, and distracting you find his requests to be.

If a likeable colleague with a genuine interest is simply testing the waters, there's probably no reason to go after him with a harpoon. Although many people do date working colleagues, others avoid the practice because of the potentially painful and awkward consequences if the relationship doesn't work out. You can let Romeo down gently but firmly by smiling ruefully and saying, "I appreciate the offer, but I make it a practice not to date people I work with. You're a nice person and I'm sure you'll respect my needs in this regard." This statement may be repeated, with minimal variations, as needed. However, if more than a couple of repetitions are required, it's time to intensify your message.

A colleague who pushes attentions on you after you've made the point that you don't return his (or her) interest is crossing the border into sexual harassment. Most people these days are aware that directing repeated, unwanted, intrusive sexual attentions at their co-workers is illegal and potentially hazardous to their own occupational welfare. You would be justified in reporting such behavior to your supervisor and/or human resources representative. It is crucial, however, that you make it clear to the pursuer that the attentions are unwelcome. Say it clearly and directly: "I insist that you stop making these personal remarks to me." "I don't appreciate this behavior, and I want it to stop right now." "I will report this behavior if it continues." It is also a good idea to keep a log of these instances of your colleague's inappropriate behavior, including a notation of any witnesses.

When the Boss Is a Bully

Q:

"My supervisor is downright rude and abusive. He yells at people, belittles us in front of others, and even calls people names like "goof-off" and "slob." Nobody likes him, and he doesn't care. Everyone is afraid to stand up to him, including me. But he's turning me into a nervous wreck, and I don't believe anyone has the right to bully people this way."

 Coaching Tip

You have the right not to remain silent.

A: It's an abuse of power to treat subordinates with blatant disrespect, and it's lousy management to boot. If there is divine, or corporate, justice, someone from above will intervene, but don't count on it. Recognize that you have the right to speak up.

There are two possible levels of response (three, if you count finding another job). At the corporate level, you might want to build the documentation to present this to human resources as a case of harassment. Keeping a log of specific incidents of abusive behavior, along with those who witnessed them, or even taping one of your boss's exhibitions could be helpful. At the personal level, your challenge is to calmly state to your supervisor that his behavior is unacceptable and to tell him what you would like him to do instead and why. We know that this seems like a very tall order. Many people are convinced that they cannot do this with a supervisor under any circumstances. A calm, clear, firm, but respectful statement of how you wish to be treated is not only appropriate, but necessary when you are being bullied. Bullies thrive on willing victims.

So take a deep breath, look the boss in the eye, and quietly say, "Please tell me calmly what you want so I can listen clearly." Nothing in that statement is insubordinate. If your boss protests or argues, repeat yourself, in the same or slightly different words.

In approaching your boss, a question to consider is whether or not you may find safety in numbers. When you know that other colleagues have similar feelings about his behavior, you may want to seek their support and address your boss together. On the other hand, being approached by a group is undoubtedly more threatening to your boss and could trigger his defenses. We suggest you start with the individual approach and consider seeking allies only if your own efforts are unsuccessful.

Dealing with an Underachiever

Q:

"I have a direct report who is frequently late to work, doesn't volunteer for any new projects, and seems to put in minimum effort on the job. I knew he was having some personal problems, and I tried to be very understanding. I counseled him and referred him to the employee assistance program (EAP), and his mood seems better. But he still comes late to work and he's not being as productive as he could be. How should I deal with him?"

Coaching Tip

Insanity is repeating the same behavior and expecting a different result.

Your understanding approach and referral to the employee assistance program were appropriate, but it now sounds like the two of you are stuck in a rut.

Instead of waiting for him to change, take the initiative and try a new approach. We call this "shifting gears."

Sometimes shifting gears in a stalled relationship can mean backing off, or taking a positive approach by reinforcing and encouraging the person, or taking time to build rapport and establish trust. But you've done that. In this situation, you can shift gears by being firmer and more consistent about what you expect from your direct report. You might say something like this:

> *"Let's make sure we're on the same page. Tell me exactly what you need to do differently in order to keep your job."* [You listen and respond to his list.] *"Good. You are clear about what I expect of you. So starting tomorrow, when you arrive at work on time, you and I will have a five-minute meeting in which you'll outline your agenda for the day. At the end of the day, we'll have another five-minute meeting to review what you've accomplished. Is that clear?"*

You then need to follow through with the plan and be consistent in your expectations and feedback. There's no guarantee that this person will shape up, but it definitely wasn't going to happen the other way.

When a Co-worker Fails to Follow Through

Q:

"One of my co-workers promised to get me some figures for an important presentation, but didn't come through. I had made the request well in advance, and she swore up and down to deliver the data. How can I deal with this kind of situation?"

 Coaching Tip

If at first they don't succeed . . .
persist, persist, persist.

A: Unfortunately, it's not all that unusual to encounter people who don't deliver on their promises. Persistence is the key to inducing them to follow through. But don't confuse persistence with nagging. People who nag are usually expressing defeat and frustration. Persistence, on the other hand, involves some strategy. Here are four strategic approaches to encouraging others to follow through.

Explore. When someone fails to deliver on a promise, calmly ask why, without attacking or criticizing. Invite them to tell you what they (or you) can do to help them follow through next time ("Joan, I'm wondering how it happened that you didn't get me the figures you promised for my presentation. . . . Next time a situation like this comes up, what do you think might help you remember?").

Remind. When you have reason to anticipate that someone may fail to follow through, take the initiative to repeat your expectation regularly. Do this without any criticism or "edge" in your voice (otherwise you're nagging). Express appreciation for any encouraging efforts ("Joan, just a reminder that my presentation is this Friday. How are you coming on those figures? Good, I'm glad to hear it's on your 'to do' list. I'll check back with you on Wednesday to see how it's coming.").

Request. In contrast to reminding, a request puts the onus on the other person to work out an action plan. Deliver your request by stating what the unacceptable behavior is, then asking what the person is willing to do about it ("Joan, the presentation is tomorrow, and you haven't given me the figures you promised. What are you willing to do at this point?"). Respond to an acceptable offer with words like "I appreciate your promise and I'm counting on you to keep it." If the person dismisses you, repeat yourself ("I mean it, Joan. Are you willing to make an effort to follow through on the commitment you made to me?").

Encourage. Teachers have a saying: *"Catch 'em doing something right,"* which reflects the fact that positive reinforcement is a more reliable motivator than punishment. If you see your co-worker take any actions that are steps in the right direction, express appreciation, without exaggerating or effusing ("Joan, Martin mentioned to me that you were asking him about where you can find the figures I asked for. I'm glad you're looking into it for me.").

Your efforts at persistence will increase the likelihood of others taking your requests seriously.

When the Boss Asks You to Do Something Unethical

Q:

"My supervisor is pushing me to do something that I'm sure is unprofessional, if not downright illegal. I feel like I'm risking my job if I refuse, but maybe risking my career and reputation if I comply. How do I handle this no-win situation?"

Coaching Tip

When your boss's position is fragile, handle with care.

A: You've just given the classic definition of a dilemma: a choice between two highly unpleasant options. No one feels good when facing such a situation. Your first critical step is to make the right decision for yourself. Do you need to do any further research to determine the ethical and/or legal implications of what your boss is asking? Or do you know that what he or she is proposing is wrong? It takes courage to speak up, and these days courage appears to be a scarce commodity in corporate America. Assuming you've concluded that you must refuse, congratulations on your integrity. Now let's look at how you might present your decision to your boss.

There are four important elements to include in addressing your supervisor:

Presume his/her innocence. Approach your boss from the assumption that he or she is acting unwittingly and doesn't realize the ethical implications or consequences. This may actually be true. Instead of accusing or blaming, acknowledge the reasons that make the proposed course of action appeal to your boss.

Use descriptive language. Avoid using loaded words like "illegal," "can't," or "outrageous." Instead, try to outline the likely consequences of the proposed action for the boss, for you, and for the organization.

Be supportive. Try to use "we" language and share the boss's concerns about the situation. Show that you understand why he or she wants to find a way to resolve the problem.

Offer alternatives. If you can, suggest ways to address the issue without risking legal or ethical problems. Suggest others who might be consulted or included in the decision.

Incorporating these four elements, you would say to your boss something like this:

"Sarah, in practical terms, what you're proposing makes a lot of sense. We do need to take some action. But we might have some problems if we do it this way. For one thing, it could give the appearance that we . . . What if we were to consider . . . instead? We could run both ideas by Roger in the legal department and see what he thinks."

If your boss remains adamant about charting an ethically perilous course, you may have to abandon ship. Seek support and counsel from human resources, professional organizations, or an attorney, as needed.

When Someone Tells Offensive Jokes

Q:

"I have a customer who likes to tell racist jokes. When he does this, I feel like vanishing into the earth. I'm terribly uncomfortable and don't want to be a party to his prejudice, but I also don't want to lose a customer. Should I speak up? If so, how?"

Coaching Tip

You don't have to swallow anything that makes you sick.

A: Many people feel torn in situations like this. No one wants to risk offending a customer, but to remain silent is to convey complicity with his racism. If this prospect disgusts you, then good for you. Beyond the issue of basic decency, prejudice is both dangerous and out of date in the modern world. In case your customer hasn't noticed, America is growing more racially diverse by the year. One of these days your customer will tell a racist joke to someone who will respond, "Perhaps you didn't know that my mother is African American. And my father is Polish."

If you decide to speak up, do so privately with the customer (in public, such jokes are best met with a stony silence). In a low-key way, tell him or her that this type of "humor" makes you uncomfortable and request that he or she not tell jokes like this in your presence. In all likelihood, the customer will apologize and back down. If not, either quietly reiterate your discomfort or say, "Perhaps you didn't know about my mother . . ."

If you prefer the indirect approach, you might respond to the offensive joke with a blank stare and say, "I don't get it." The person will probably repeat the so-called punchline and you can ask, "Why is that funny?" The person will get the message. However, the indirect approach has the potential to make him or her more embarrassed and uncomfortable. You might want to reserve this method for former customers.

Once in a while, you may get a rejoinder like "Hey, don't take it personally. It's just a joke." Keep cool and say, "I'm sure you don't want to hurt my feelings. Are you willing to respect my preferences and spare me this type of humor?" Respond to any sort of affirmative answer, however grudging, with thanks.

Strategy 4:

Invite Others to Be Your Mirror Rather than Your Blind Spot

Consider each of the following hypothetical work situations. Would you want others to tell you if the situation were true of you? Would you be likely to tell someone else if the situation were true of him or her?

- ❑ Giving a presentation with a piece of spinach stuck between your teeth
- ❑ Writing poor-quality business letters
- ❑ Not appearing as energetic as you used to
- ❑ Mispronouncing a customer's name
- ❑ Having a habit that distracts colleagues in meetings, such as jingling coins in your pocket or tapping with your pen
- ❑ Dressing inappropriately for the office

Although you probably wouldn't be happy to learn that any of these scenarios applied to you, if you are like most people, you would be more willing to *receive* such feedback (assuming it were true) than to *volunteer* it to someone else. This is the basic feedback dilemma: We all have blind spots and need others to reveal them to us, but others are often reluctant to do so.

Think of all the reasons you might hesitate to tell a colleague (or worse, your boss) that he or she was guilty of any of these faux pas. Maybe you're not sure the person would appreciate the feedback. Maybe you would be overstepping your bounds, especially if the person is your boss. Maybe he or she would get angry, or even seek reprisal. Maybe you just don't want the hassle.

Because honest feedback on the job is an important and scarce commodity, people-smart individuals have learned that waiting for it isn't enough. Instead, they practice the strategy of inviting feedback from a wide circle of people. Even when they disagree with the feedback they receive, people-smart individuals know that they are better off knowing how others see them than guessing.

Many companies have policies mandating 360-degree feedback (that is, feedback from supervisors, peers, and direct reports), often in the form of surveys completed annually or quarterly. Although this is clearly a step in the right direction, people-smart individuals don't just rely on a formal policy. They also take the initiative to seek out ongoing "feedback relationships" with others in their work lives.

In a feedback relationship, there is a shared commitment to exchange perspectives about each other's performance and about the relationship. Both parties feel free to offer and request input from one another. Imagine having genuine, spontaneous 360-degree feedback relationships at work. Consider what some of the benefits might be:

- ❏ Not having to guess what others really think about your work
- ❏ Getting a wide enough sample of opinion to recognize trends (as well as input that's off the wall)
- ❏ Learning who tends to give the most helpful feedback on specific issues, so that you know whom to approach about what
- ❏ Hearing more praise than you are accustomed to
- ❏ Getting more ideas and suggestions to help you improve
- ❏ Feeling closer to the people you work with
- ❏ Getting some things off your chest instead of keeping them to yourself

 Coaching Contract

Think about the people you deal with at work. From which of them do you routinely receive feedback? Among those who don't share frequent (or perhaps any) feedback with you, which of them might have a perspective worth hearing?

Most of us don't experience consistent feedback relationships on the job. And yet all of that information is out there, just waiting to be harvested—if we can learn how to ask for it convincingly. Unfortunately, feedback requests often come across as superficial, or worse, as fishing for compliments. Consider this exchange between Alan, who has just concluded a presentation to his clients, and Paige, his assistant:

Alan: *How was the presentation?*

Paige: (hesitates) *You did . . . great.*

Alan: *Paige, you seem a little hesitant. Are you sure I didn't bore them?*

Paige: (trying to sound convincing) *No, honestly, you were really great. I think they loved it.*

Alan: *Good, I thought I nailed it!*

Afraid to give Alan any criticism, Paige withholds her true opinions and offers him bland reassurances, which Alan is only too eager to embrace. But what if the clients didn't think much of his presentation either? By missing out on constructive feedback, Alan loses an opportunity to correct course. Consider how Paige might have responded if Alan's feedback request had sounded like this:

> "Paige, I'm concerned about the future of this account, because I'm picking up signals that they're not fully happy with our services. I would really appreciate your honest impressions of how that presentation went. In particular, I'd like to hear how you think I handled their questions at the end, because, frankly, I'm not sure I really understood their concerns. If you'd rather not just answer off the top of your head, how about giving it some thought and getting back to me with your feedback later today?"

Better, right? Let's zero in on the success strategies that make this a more people-smart feedback invitation.

Four Ways to Encourage Feedback

Here are four S's (that's "S" as in "success") to keep in mind when you are seeking quality feedback from others. Incorporate these elements in order to reduce people's discomfort and improve the chances of getting their honest and constructive input.

1 Sincerity.

Present an authentic rationale for wanting someone's feedback.

- ❏ *"I'm serious about improving my meeting facilitation skills, and you could really help me by sharing some of your thoughts about how I led the meeting we just had."*

- ❏ *"You have a lot of experience with this equipment and I'm new at this. Would you be willing to watch me while I try to operate it and tell me how I'm doing?"*

2 Specificity

Be clear about the particular feedback you are seeking.

- ❏ *"Would you please tell me when you notice me interrupting others?"*

- ❏ *"What do you think I could have done differently to try to handle that customer?"*

3 Safety.

Avoid putting others on the spot when you ask them for feedback. In fact, go the extra mile to make them comfortable. Sometimes it helps to change the scene and talk over a lunch table instead of a conference table. Give others time to prepare their feedback, or even offer anonymity when appropriate.

- ❏ *"I'd really like your feedback about how I handled this presentation. Would you be willing to get back to me later this week with your thoughts?"*

- ❏ *"When we meet with Lucy this afternoon, would you please observe how well I do at dealing with her anxieties and give me your comments and suggestions afterward?"*

Start the process by acknowledging some of your own flaws as a way to model and give permission for honest feedback.

❑ *"I thought I was pretty patient with Ron's objections, but I'm not sure I did a very good job supporting our views. What did you think?"*

❑ *"I feel like I'm getting more comfortable with these cold calls, but I wonder if I could do better at closing the sale."*

 Coaching Contract

How might you use one or more of these strategies to invite someone in your work life to give you useful feedback?

The Power of Positive Feedback

Whether or not you agree with the feedback others give in response to your requests, be sure to thank them for being willing to share it with you. You may have heard the adage "Feedback is a gift." Bear in mind that it is also a gift you can "return to the store" if it just doesn't fit.

A concern that people in organizations frequently raise is the difficulty of getting positive feedback from supervisors. Too often, managers adopt an attitude of "no news is good news," expecting silence to be interpreted as satisfaction. We've even heard the explicit view that "professionals shouldn't need to be praised for doing a good job."

We think this is misguided.

Psychologists have long known that reward is a more powerful tool than punishment when the goal is to shape behavior. Teachers have a saying, "Catch 'em doing something right," that applies the same principle. Positive feedback isn't just a way to make people feel good; it's a powerful motivator. When you pinpoint something an individual has done well and ask for more of the same, you are providing valuable information. Withhold the feedback and you waste an opportunity.

Can you request positive feedback from your boss without sounding needy? We think so. One way to do this is to use the teacher trick and capitalize on the situation if your boss does happen to volunteer a compliment. Thank him or her and add, "Your feedback means a lot to me. I find I learn even more when you point out what I'm doing that's on target. I hope you won't mind if I ask you to share more of those reactions in the future." Among the four S's, sincerity is probably key in requesting positive feedback from above. Help your boss recognize that you're not just fishing for compliments but are seeking to fine-tune your performance when you solicit his or her feedback.

When It's Your Turn to Be the Mirror

People-smart individuals also know how to give feedback in a sensitive and skillful way. If you think about it, being a frequent feedback recipient attunes you to how it feels to be on the receiving end and helps you become more conscious of how your own feedback may be experienced by others. It's better to offer feedback provisionally than as a pronouncement. Let your words and tone convey that, after all, it's an opinion you are sharing, rather than one of the ten commandments. When they have occasion to share feedback, here are the strategies that people-smart individuals practice. You don't have to use all of them, but consider which ones you might want to practice more often:

① Ask permission.

Before plunging ahead, check to see if the other person is ready and willing to hear you out.

❑ *"Is this a good time for me to tell you some thoughts I have about . . . ?"*

❑ *"Would you be open to hearing some feedback about . . . ?"*

② Compliment first.

Start by reflecting something you genuinely value or appreciate about the person–especially something relevant to the subject of your feedback.

❑ *"You have a warm, friendly tone with the customers you call."*

❑ *"You obviously did your homework. You had plenty of facts to back up your project status report."*

Focus on behavior. Describe specific actions, rather than labeling the person. Give examples when possible.

❑ *"It seems to me that you tend to focus on the negative rather than the positive when you conduct performance appraisals. For instance, just now, you told Mr. Jones . . . "*

❑ *"There were a couple of times when, in your eagerness to share your data, you may have misunderstood the client's question. Remember when Claire asked about . . . ?"*

③ Offer suggestions.

Give one or two concrete recommendations for improvement. This way you are focusing on the future, not the past. Make sure your suggestions are doable for the person.

❏ *"Perhaps before making sales calls you could write up a little crib sheet to remind yourself of possible benefits you can mention."*

❏ *"If you paraphrase the question before you start to answer it, you can check whether you've got a handle on the person's real concern."*

Ask for reactions. Check to see if the person understands and agrees with your feedback. Correct any misimpressions she or he may have received.

❏ *"Do you feel that this is true?"*

❏ *"Is this helpful?"*

❏ *"How do you see it?"*

❏ *"Is that okay with you?"*

When you take the time to give feedback in a careful and caring way, others are more likely to listen and consider what you say to them. They may also be more likely to make an effort to give you quality feedback in return.

Coaching Contract

Select a person at work for whom you have some potentially valuable feedback. What are some phrases you might use to share your views with him or her?

And now let's turn to some work scenarios where people-smart feedback exchanges can help promote success—up, down, and side by side.

Coaxing Praise Out of a Stony Boss

Q:

"My boss doesn't believe in giving praise. Her attitude is that if she doesn't complain about my work, I should know she's satisfied. But I feel a need for more specific feedback about what I'm doing right. How can I convey this to her without sounding needy?"

Coaching Tip

Positive feedback builds performance.

The key to persuading your boss to give you more positive feedback lies in the rationale you give for your request. Give her a genuine reason why you want her feedback. Don't say (or convey), "I want your feedback because my pitiful, shriveled ego is starving for praise." It also won't help to adopt an injured tone ("I work so hard and you never seem to acknowledge it"). Instead present a sincere reason that involves a benefit to her or to the organization. Here are some examples.

"Maybe you don't realize how helpful your feedback is to me. Even when I do something well, I don't always understand exactly what was right about it. When you clarify this for me, it takes away the guesswork and helps me to be more consistent in my performance."

"I'd like to build on my strengths. You usually have excellent suggestions about how I can apply my successes to new areas. Maybe I could take on some new projects and reduce some of the load on others."

"Sometimes I'm pretty hard on myself. If I know you're happy with the work I'm producing, I'll be less likely to waste my energy worrying about it and I'll probably be more productive."

If your boss still resists, don't become defensive. Calmly reiterate your request and look for a way to get your "foot in the door" without expecting your boss to make a total or permanent commitment. Perhaps your boss would agree to share some positive feedback about a specific project you completed, or for a trial period of a few weeks. Maybe she would be willing to e-mail some favorable comments to you if she doesn't have time to meet in person. If she resists even these small steps, you might say, "I understand that my request is inconvenient for you, but it's really important to me. I hope you'll at least agree to give it some further thought."

When a Team Is Short on Feedback

Q:

"*Sometimes it seems like the more work I put in, the less I get back from my teammates. When I most want and need constructive feedback, I'm usually disappointed at how little they offer or how off-the-wall the feedback I do get from them is. How can I coax some useful feedback out of them?*"

Coaching Tip

Feedback is a gift, but sometimes you have to let people know what you want and what size you wear.

A: There are many reasons people are reluctant to give honest feedback, including fear of reprisals or hurting someone's feelings, uncertainty about what to say, or feeling unqualified to give an opinion. As if these barriers weren't enough, there is also the possibility that your teammates may be jealous of your work or too invested in the outcome of your ideas to be objective.

In spite of these obstacles, there are some things you can do to encourage quality feedback from your team:

Seek feedback widely. Consider broadening the cross-section of people whose feedback you request. Most of us have blind spots—people we just don't think of approaching for feedback. Perhaps there are support staff, clients, or individuals outside your team who can offer you a fresh perspective.

Give a compelling rationale. Let people know why you need their feedback and how it could be helpful to you, and possibly to them. You might tell your teammates, "If this presentation goes poorly, I'm afraid we'll all find ourselves swimming upstream with this client. I really need your suggestions about how to perk it up."

Structure the feedback you want. Be specific about the kind of feedback that will be helpful and make it easy for others to give it. Instead of asking, "What do you think of my presentation?" you might ask, "I'm afraid this presentation is running too long. Where would you suggest I might cut it?" Consider developing a brief feedback checklist or questionnaire to distribute or e-mail to your teammates, giving them a deadline to complete and return it.

Finally, if some of the feedback you get seems off-the-wall, thank the person anyway and don't dismiss their feedback completely. Sift through it for any nuggets of truth worth salvaging.

When a Staff Member Needs Grooming

Q:

"I'm a project leader, and one of the junior members of my team could use a serious makeover. Dean is a sweet guy and we all love his quirky sense of humor. But he looks like a refugee from Woodstock! I mean, the guy actually wears shoulder-length hair and Birkenstocks to the office. Sometimes he even wears his nose ring to work. People joke about his grooming, and I feel like it's my responsibility to say something to him. How do I talk about something as personal as grooming without offending him?"

 Coaching Tip

Your feedback might hurt for a moment but prevent years of pain.

A: Good for you that you're willing to step up to the plate. This person's style deficits could jeopardize his career prospects. As his supervisor, you owe it to him to offer constructive feedback. The key elements that make feedback effective are to ask permission. start with a genuine compliment, be specific and descriptive, offer suggestions for improvement, and check out the person's reactions. Let's see how you might apply this formula to Dean's situation.

Start with "Dean, we've been working together quite a while. Would you be open to some personal feedback?" If you pick up any discomfort, acknowledge this: "You look a bit hesitant." Tell him, "I'm really happy with your work. I enjoy working with you and I see you as someone who always goes the extra mile to do a good job. I'd like to think you have a future here, and, in that spirit, I want to offer a suggestion."

Now cut to the chase: "Your style is kind of hip in its way, but it's not making you look like a contender in this corner of corporate America. Do you have a sense of what I'm getting at?" Listen and be supportive of his response. If he seems surprised, hurt, or defensive, acknowledge this before moving on. "Can I give you a couple of examples? The nose ring, for instance, may be a distraction for people . . ." Invite him to consider how others, perhaps at higher levels, are dressing for success at work.

If he seems defensive, don't push. Instead, say something like "I hope this doesn't seem out of line. I could be wrong, but I'm in your corner and I honestly believe this is something important for you to think about." If this doesn't work, see if the "Fab Five" is available to give Dean a makeover.

Delivering Your Resignation

Q:

"I've been fed up with my job for a long time, mainly because the CEO has made my life miserable since he's been in charge. Now I've found a great new opportunity and I can move on, on my own terms. I'm delighted and can't wait to see his face when I tell him I'm leaving. I'd like to tell him the truth about why I'm quitting and let him know what I think of some of his ridiculous decisions and disastrous policies. I really don't see how he can do anything to hurt me. What do you think—bombs away?"

A: First of all, ask yourself, "what's my goal?" Are you seeking revenge or a chance to make some valid points about the way he's run the organization?

Dropping the big one may feel satisfying, but he'll undoubtedly tune you out And even if he can't retaliate against you directly, how will your criticism affect his treatment of the people, policies, and programs you leave behind as your legacy? You may just be giving him the excuse to scapegoat those who were loyal to you and to dismantle your accomplishments.

Instead of dropping a bomb, you might treat your resignation as an opportunity to offer him some constructive feedback about one or two of his more dubious practices. To do this effectively, you could start the process in one of two ways. One is to say something like "I know it's not always easy to get people's honest perspective when you're the boss. Would you be open to some feedback from a departing direct report?" It's hard to say no to this question without looking like a total creep. The other opening is to ask him to give you some parting feedback about your performance, listen, thank him, and then ask if you might reciprocate. Again, to refuse would be extremely rude.

Once you're in the door, use the principles of giving effective feedback. Start by sharing something genuine and positive (yes, you'll need to give this a lot of thought). Then say "I think you could be even more effective if you were to . . ." and identify just one or two key behaviors he could change. Offer examples and specific suggestions. Then be sure to check out his reactions to what you've shared. Wish him well and walk out—on the high ground.

Dealing with Gossip

Q:

"I overheard one of my direct reports, Jerry, talking to a co-worker and making some very disparaging remarks about another member of the team, Lou. I don't know whether to just ignore it or to mention it to Jerry."

Coaching Tip

Try to convert gossip into feedback.

A: If you want to discourage gossip in your work group, there are two approaches you might consider: the public route and the private route. If you opt for the first, you can essentially make a public service announcement at a team meeting, along these lines:

"I want our team to have a policy of open and honest communication with each other. This means that we ask for and share feedback with each other directly. It also means that we don't hold back feedback that could be constructive, or turn it into gossip, which isn't constructive. What do the rest of you think about this goal?"

Allow them to react and discuss. If they appear to be in agreement (and this is a difficult goal to oppose, at least openly), say, "Good. Can we agree to hold each other accountable to this goal?" Now you have a clear and legitimate mandate to confront the next gossiper you overhear. When it happens, use it as a teaching opportunity and model the kind of constructive feedback you're encouraging:

"I've been hearing some grumbling about the fact that Lou got the promotion to the vacant project manager position. It's no secret that several people on the team applied. I realize it's a sensitive subject, but I'd like us to clear the air. I'm going to say a little about what I believe Lou will bring to the position, and I want you all to raise any questions you have about the selection process, either right now in the meeting or one-on-one with me."

Whether or not you go public, you can meet individually with Jerry to discuss his, and your, concerns. Tell him you overheard his conversation about Lou, and ask him point-blank whether he has any concerns about Lou or his work performance that he thinks you should be aware of. In all likelihood, he will back down and say no. In that case, you can tell him you just wanted to check, because if there is a problem, you want to be in a position to deal with it. It's just possible that Jerry does have some legitimate concerns. If so, you can decide whether the appropriate action is to speak with Lou yourself or redirect Jerry to raise his concerns directly with Lou. Either way, your message is that feedback is *constructive,* whereas gossip is *destructive.*

Opening a "Clam"

Q:

"One of my direct reports just won't open up and share opinions, even when I ask. Her favorite response is 'I don't know.' Her work is good, so I know she's not stupid. How can I get more input from her?"

 Coaching Tip

To pry open a clam, apply gradual pressure.

A: The common mistake is to repeat variations of the question that didn't work. A better approach is to use less threatening follow-up questions and approaches that elicit kernels of response, and then build on them.

When your direct report says, "I don't know," try coming back with questions that are more focused and specific, such as

- ❑ *"Well, if you were to hazard a guess, which part of the proposal sounds best to you?"*
- ❑ *"What do you think is making it hard for you to give an opinion on this?"*
- ❑ *"How did you feel about the last part of the presentation?"*

An even more basic question to start with is a direct one that requires her only to answer yes or no ("Did that opening work for you?"). Remember, your initial goal is to get her started and be able to thank her for sharing something.

Some variations on the follow-up question include offering perspectives, rationales, and structure as ways to elicit feedback:

Perspective. Share your point of view before asking hers ("I thought our data could have been stronger. What do you think?"). This signals to her that you are open to constructive criticism.

Rationale. Give a genuine and compelling reason why you want her input ("I've been writing this report so long that I've lost perspective. Your fresh vision could be invaluable to me at this point.").

Structure. Make it easier for her to provide input by offering checklists or e-mailing questions. Instead of putting the person on the spot, give her time to gather her thoughts and get back to you.

Reinforce any feedback you do get by thanking the person and letting her know exactly how the feedback was helpful to you.

When Your Boss Gives You a Verbal Warning

Q:

"My supervisor just told me she's not satisfied with my job performance. She said this constitutes an official verbal warning that my work must improve. I can't afford to lose this job. Is it too late to salvage the situation?"

Coaching Tip

A crisis represents both danger and opportunity.

A: Not if you take the warning seriously. In the progressive discipline process, a verbal warning is the first step, which may be followed by a written warning and then dismissal. Think of this as Condition Orange and put yourself on high alert. Here is a three-step plan that can help you save your job.

Get clear on expectations. Ask your boss for feedback about her specific concerns regarding your job performance, including examples of recent work products and behavior that haven't measured up to her standards. Encourage her to spell out her expectations for improvement. Ask questions like "What key behaviors would indicate to you that I was meeting or surpassing your expectations?" You might also ask her if she can suggest a colleague whom you might consider as a role model, so that you can observe how this person handles similar responsibilities. Take careful notes and send your supervisor an e-mail memo summarizing what you understand to be her concerns and expectations.

Take a serious inventory. Once you've gotten clear with your supervisor, get clear with yourself about where the real problem lies. Have you simply not understood what your supervisor expects of you? If not, why not? Do you need to work on improving your ongoing communication with your boss? Or is the problem that you lack some specific knowledge or skills needed to do the job well? Perhaps there's a training program or resource that can help you get up to speed. Have you been sabotaging your own work out of some sort of resistance to the job or the boss? Try examining your basic assumptions and feelings about your work situation, including what makes you happy and unhappy about being there. Counseling or coaching may help with this process. Unless you are prepared to make a real commitment to changing your attitude or behavior, you're probably heading for Condition Red.

Establish a feedback loop. Ask your supervisor to meet with you regularly to review your progress. As in step 1, take notes during these meetings and send your supervisor summaries of the feedback and action plans you agree on.

Treat this verbal warning as a wake-up call. It's time to either go the extra mile to keep the job you have or start searching for the job you really want. Or maybe both.

Handling a Chronic Complainer

Q:

"Someone on my staff is extremely negative. He responds to every request with a complaint, even in team meetings. Everyone notices his behavior, and it's having a negative effect on morale. What can I do?"

 Coaching Tip

Freedom of speech has its limits.

A: A team member who chronically airs complaints is like a loudspeaker broadcasting dirges in the office. It brings everyone down. And you're the one who needs to deal with it. Meet with Mr. Negativity one-on-one and offer him a mixture of one part empathy and two parts firmness in your feedback.

Start by exploring whether he is even aware of his complaining ("Gary, I've been noticing that you seem to respond to requests from the team with complaints. Are you aware that you've been doing this?"). Give some acknowledgement and support: "I hate to see you so unhappy. I do value your contributions to the team." Then specify the problem and suggest alternatives:

> *"When your automatic response is to complain, it creates two problems. It pushes others away and it spreads negativity like a dark cloud. Neither of these results helps you or the team. If you are feeling overwhelmed here, let's sort out the problems you're having and see how we can resolve them."*

Check out his response to your feedback by asking a question like "Am I making sense?" or "Do you have any questions or reactions to what I've just said?"

Make sure your complainer understands that you want him to come to you directly with his concerns, rather than air them in front of the team. Acknowledge any efforts he makes to correct his behavior ("Gary, I appreciate your accepting that new assignment so graciously. It was a big help.").

Strategy 5:

Be Open to Resistance Rather than Fight It

For most of us, the idea of being open to resistance is akin to welcoming a head cold. But it is one of life's paradoxes that the times when we are most eager to push our own causes are the very times when we must be most receptive to counter-arguments. Who ever said life was fair?

To grasp this paradox, consider Newton's Law: Every action has an equal and opposite reaction. Pushing back is a law of nature. In the martial arts, an expert puts this to his advantage by using an opponent's own force to topple him. As another analogy, consider what it takes to hold on to a handful of sand: The more tightly you grasp, the faster the sand slips away. Often the best way to counteract resistance is to drop our barriers.

It isn't unusual to encounter resistance in the work world. It waits for us at the other end of the telephone line when we call a customer. You can spot it in the skeptical expression of your boss as he or she listens to your proposal. It echoes in the "*yes, but . . .*" of a direct report facing a tight deadline. In virtually any situation involving conflict or any encounter in which we hope to persuade another, success depends on how adroitly we handle resistance.

People-Smart Persuasion

Resistance is always part of the picture in situations where we want to influence the thoughts, feelings, and actions of others. When others already agree with you, persuasion is unnecessary. There's a maxim in sales: "*When the customer says no, that's when the selling starts.*" But you don't need to be a sales rep to "sell." All of us are in the business of promoting our ideas, beliefs, needs, and values to those around us at work. Managing up is probably 90% influencing. What else can we do? When one can't command, one can only try to persuade

Even when one is nominally in command, influence is essential. Managers can generate assignments and directives until their voices give out and their fingers fall off. The ones who get results are those who induce their people to buy in. For example, we found that supervisors in an oil refinery who persuaded their employees to be safety conscious were much more effective than those supervisors who "ordered" employees to heed safety procedures.

Try this exercise in selling: Make your best effort to convince someone to try a particular product or service you really like, but do so *without asking the other person any questions.* Even if you are enthusiastic and compelling in your presentation, you will probably achieve only partial success. And yet this is exactly what most of us tend to do. We let our enthusiasm carry us along, only to discover that we've left our "buyer" behind.

When people don't think or do willingly what we want them to, we need to drop our own agenda for a while to learn about the other person's needs, concerns, and objections. That's what it means to be open to resistance. By uncovering what matters to the other person, we gain the ability to present our ideas in terms that may hold particular appeal to him or her. And in this sense, resistance provides a real opportunity. Someone who is willing to come out and tell us his or her concerns or objections is giving us material to work with. In contrast, silent acquiescence provides only a false sense of security.

 Coaching Contract

Think of a recent situation in which you were unsuccessful in persuading a customer, colleague, employee, or boss to adopt your agenda.
Consider the approach you used and ask yourself the following three questions. Based on your self-assessment, what would you do differently if you were to face the same or a similar situation in the future?

❑ **Did I ask questions to better understand the person's perspective?**

Skillful questions can help you obtain useful information (see Goldberg-Adams, 2004, *Change Your Questions, Change Your Life,* (San Francisco: Berrett-Koehler). Did you try to find out what needs or problems the person was facing? What they had already done to try to solve the problems? Did you invite their reactions to the ideas you were putting forth?

❑ **Did I point out the benefits the person would receive by adopting my agenda?**

Sales experts distinguish between "features" (the general attributes of a product or service) and "benefits" (the personal value of the product/service to an individual). With respect to benefits, one size does *not* fit all. Some large companies offer the *feature* of an in-house fitness center. However, employees may experience the *benefits* of this resource in different ways. Some, for example, may find that exercising during their lunch breaks is a stress-buster. Others may enjoy the social opportunities available when they work out at the end of the day. If you didn't ask the kind of questions we just considered, you probably were hard-pressed to suggest compelling benefits for your prospect.

❑ **Did I give the person time and space to mull over my proposal?**

Patience is a critical quality in persuasion. Faced with resistance, many people become anxious or impatient. Their instincts are either to push harder or to give up. Being open to resistance often requires biding your time and being prepared to renew your efforts at a later date when circumstances may make the other person more ready to consider your ideas.

In seeking the difficult balance point between patience and pursuit, it helps to get a foot in the door. Instead of pushing for a big "yes," request a small one by trying one or more of these strategies:

❑ Ask the person to merely listen to your suggestion and do not expect a response.

❑ Invite the person to read something relevant to your recommendation.

- ❑ Encourage the person to try out your suggestion as a one-time experiment.
- ❑ Urge the person to consider only one part of your recommendation rather than the whole enchilada.

All of these foot-in-the-door approaches represent ways for you to keep your cause alive while respecting the other person's resistance. Here is an example.

A supervisor was urging a group of tollbooth collectors to be friendlier to drivers when they paid the tolls. The collectors resisted. "If we talk like they do in stores and hotels these days," they argued, "the public will think we're crazy or just forced to do it. It's not what people expect." The supervisor wisely responded, "Okay, I'll make a deal with you. Try to say hello or thank you, or smile to the customers for one week, and we'll get back together to see if it works." The next week the toll collectors reported that they did not know what effect the experiment had had on the customers, but they all reported that they liked their jobs better.

(No doubt the customers returned their friendliness in kind.)

Disarming Criticism

Sometimes others will not merely resist you but will attack back. It's almost impossible to view someone's angry response as a learning opportunity. When someone reacts to you in an attacking manner, it's difficult to appreciate the wealth of valuable information coming your way. Even under these conditions, however, the principle of being open to resistance applies. Once again, there is a paradox at work. If you disagree with a bit of angry criticism, even if it is untrue and unfair, you make the criticism look valid. In contrast, if you genuinely accept the criticism, however untrue and unfair, you instantly put the lie to it. Consider this example:

Maggie is a patent attorney and a partner in a midsize firm. Although the partners pride themselves on being collaborative, there are times when competition and self-interest prevail. Maggie, who has an outspoken style, has had several clashes with fellow partners. Her complaints have ranged from being left out of the information loop to learning that other partners were pursuing litigation activities in direct conflict with her patent prosecutions.

Yesterday Maggie learned that three other partners met with her biggest patent client to pursue venture investing business, without informing or making any effort to include her. Outraged, Maggie sent an e-mail message to the managing partner describing the situation and asking, "Is this what passes for teamwork around here?"

The managing partner replied,

"I am very disappointed in your extremely self-absorbed e-mail. It reflects a deep misunderstanding of this firm, how we serve clients, how we deal with each other, and your role and obligations as a partner. Your behavior has since the very beginning been aberrant. I have given you the benefit of the doubt because you were new to the firm, but you have become a more high-maintenance individual than the firm should have to deal with."

Notice the dilemma his response poses for Maggie. He has branded her as not a team player, and if she disputes this, that is just the way she will appear. To defuse the managing partner's attack, Maggie goes to see him and says,

"It sounds like you're at the end of your rope and turning gray over my complaints. You've been trying to be fair to everyone, and it must seem like all I do is rock the boat. I realize you're very angry."

Because Maggie's response is anything but "self-absorbed," it contradicts his characterization more effectively than any defense she might offer. When the managing partner calms down, Maggie follows up by asking, "In this present situation, what is it you think I'm not recognizing?" After listening to and paraphrasing his response, she says, "Would you be willing to give me five minutes to summarize my major concerns?"

This technique is called *disarming*. It is the verbal equivalent of politely removing the gun from your assailant's hand while it's pointed at you. Here's how disarming is done.

❑ **Find the kernel of truth.** There is inevitably some shred of reality buried within the most outlandish charge. Even paranoid delusions are based on some element of truth. (In Maggie's case, although the managing partner was clearly scapegoating her, her direct and outspoken style *was* at odds with the "groupthink" of her firm.) Although your impulse will be to deny the criticism, look for some piece of it that you can genuinely acknowledge.

- ❑ **Acknowledge and empathize.** Express your recognition and respect for what the person is saying. Along with your acknowledgment of the kernel of truth, state how the person is probably feeling. If you can, validate that he or she has reason to feel that way.
- ❑ **Seek more information.** Gently probe to learn more about what the other person's feelings and concerns may be.

Only after successfully using the disarming approach should you express your disagreement or speak in your own defense. Until the person knows you've listened, he or she won't pay attention to your arguments anyway. Besides, how people-smart is it to argue with someone who's pointing a gun at you?

Disarming is perhaps the most challenging mode of being open to resistance. It requires calmness and respect during the heat of battle. Sometimes it's just too difficult to pull off. However, disarming is an incredibly powerful technique that can defuse and transform even the most highly charged encounter quickly and painlessly, clearing the air for genuine dialogue and understanding. Use this approach successfully just once and you will be convinced of its power.

Surfacing and Resolving Conflict

Resistance is inherent in conflict. When people have competing claims, it is very difficult for them to be open to each other's needs and concerns. Often people try to circumvent the discomfort of addressing conflict in an open way, attempting instead to force their solutions on others or avoid the conflict entirely (the proverbial "fight or flight" response to danger). Resistance is suppressed or ignored but still simmers below the surface. As a result, resolutions to the conflict are shallow and short-lived. When the next conflict arises, lingering resentments and mistrust may further fuel the flames.

To reach, or even attempt, a win-win solution requires a willing and active effort to understand the other person's stated—and unstated—needs. Instead of pushing prematurely for a solution, the people-smart approach is to ask good questions aimed at uncovering what is important to the other person, so that these issues can become part of the negotiating process. (Of course, we also need to think through exactly what *we* want.) The kinds of questions that can help uncover needs might include

- ❏ *"What are some of the things that are important to you in this situation?"*
- ❏ *"What makes that important for you?"*
- ❏ *"What else are you concerned about?"*
- ❏ *"What do you believe will happen if your needs/wishes are not met?"*
- ❏ *"How else could the situation be improved?"*

Armed with a fuller understanding of one another's needs and concerns, two people have more options to work with in brainstorming a mutually acceptable solution, and more assurance that the issues they address are the important ones. Even if a solution isn't currently at hand, their good-faith efforts to understand and negotiate help to preserve a respectful working relationship. It's rarely people-smart to burn bridges. You never know when you'll need to make a return trip.

Imagine a conflict between two co-workers over the length of team meetings. Carol feels strongly that meetings should start and end on time, while Jim believes the meetings should continue until people have exhausted their issues, even if that means running late. Consider how they might respond to the preceding questions.

Carol	Jim
What are some of the things that are important to you in this situation?	
"If we run late, I may miss calls or meetings with my customers."	"Issues get raised, but they don't get resolved."
What makes that important for you?	
"In this tough economy, I can't take a chance on ticking off my customers."	"I think we really have a morale problem building around here."

What else are you concerned about?

"Well, I think our meeting process could be improved. If we spent less time ventilating and more time seeking solutions, we'd be more productive and efficient."	"I think we may be spending too much time on status reports that could be circulated in writing. We should be using the face-to-face time for creative problem solving."

What do you believe will happen if your needs are not met?

"I'll probably stop scheduling customer contacts on team meeting days. It may hurt my sales figures."	"People will just give up. The best ones might just leave when they get the chance."

How else could the situation be improved?

"Couldn't we poll the team by e-mail about some of these issues ahead of time so we'd have everyone's input in front of us at the meeting?"	"Maybe we could have a full-day team meeting quarterly with a pre-set agenda so we could get into some of these issues in depth."

A little exploration shows that, in spite of their apparently opposing positions, Carol and Jim have some common concerns about the meeting process and some good suggestions that could be part of a solution (for instance, a quarterly full-day retreat, where small groups present action recommendations on specific issues, having polled group members for their perspectives ahead of time). But if you just looked at their initial positions in seeking a solution, you might end up with a half-baked compromise that wouldn't really address the key issues (like just adding a half-hour to the meeting, but making sure it ends on time).

In the business scenarios that follow, see how openness to resistance helps promote better solutions—and relationships—even when the heat is on.

Responding to a Customer's Angry E-mail Message

Q:

"A customer sent me an e-mail message that just bristled with anger. He accused me of all sorts of things, most of which sounded really off base. Should I write back and defend myself?"

 Coaching Tip

When a customer complains, be grateful.

A: Like the child who contemplated the pile of manure and exclaimed, "Oh, goody, a pony!" you can find the bright side to a customer's complaint.

There are at least two reasons to appreciate his or her negative feedback:

1. By complaining, instead of just disappearing, the customer gives you an opportunity to respond and rectify the situation.

2. It's better that the customer complains to you rather than about you, which could alienate other prospective customers.

We recommend you repeat these two statements to yourself at least twice before responding to your customer's message. But even then, don't respond until you have re-read the message and found the inevitable kernel of truth hidden within the outrageous complaints. Instead of marshaling your counter-arguments, prepare to disarm the client by empathizing and acknowledging his or her grievances.

Instead of responding via e-mail, consider approaching the customer more directly through a phone call or meeting. It has been estimated that only 7% of communication occurs through the words we say, with the other 93% being conveyed through such nonverbal nuances as body language and voice tone. In this type of situation, less is *not* more. You are better off receiving and sending more complete messages when you hash things out with the client. Also, responding in a more direct and personal manner helps demonstrate your concern for the customer. So it would be a good idea to call him or her and say, "I read your e-mail message and it's clear that you're angry about some important issues. I'd like to come over and hear more about your concerns. Are you free any time this afternoon?"

It may seem as if this approach is more time-consuming than an e-mail response, but in fact this is probably not the case. It's worth taking the time for a face-to-face meeting where you can better understand your client's concerns, show empathy, and correct any possible misconceptions. It takes a personal rather than an electronic exchange to do this properly. Save the higher technology for less charged situations.

Asking for a Raise

Q:

"I really deserve a raise, but I know my boss is going to raise objections, especially since our budget is so tight. What's the best way to ask for one?"

Coaching Tip

Everyone listens to WIFM.

A: The people-smart way to seek organizational goodies like raises, promotions, and time off is to remember that everyone's favorite radio station is WIFM—

"What's in It for Me?" Before you take your request to the boss, think through how to tailor your message to his or her needs, interests, and values. Instead of telling your boss why you *deserve* a raise (even though you undoubtedly do!), try an approach like this:

> *"I value this company and I'm committed to its success. I would really like to know that the company, in turn, sees me as someone who can make progressive contributions to the enterprise. With the economy being the way it is, I've been working a part-time second job some evenings to save for my kids' college tuition. I'd love to put those hours in here instead and take on some additional projects. Would you be open to considering giving me a raise when the budget permits?"*

Most bosses will respond more favorably to ambition, coupled with a willingness to work hard, than to entitlement. Here are some other things you might consider before approaching your boss:

- ❑ What's the best time to talk to him or her?
- ❑ What does he or she value? Success? Loyalty? Teamwork?
- ❑ What motivates him or her? Praise? Respect? Attention?
- ❑ Is he or she formal or informal?
- ❑ Does he or she prefer to schmooze or have people come right to the point?

When you speak with your boss, be calm, clear, and concise. Be prepared to give him or her time and space to mull over your request, rather than pressuring him or her for a decision. Remember that big requests, like raises and promotions, may take time to materialize. Be willing to plant some seeds and wait for them to grow.

When Customers Don't Return Calls

Q:

"I'm an independent contractor and have to bring in business in order to survive. Often, after getting initial inquiries from prospective customers, I end up calling back and leaving numerous messages for them, without their ever returning my calls. It's incredibly frustrating. It reminds me of high school dating, sitting around waiting for the phone to ring! So how can I encourage them to call?"

 Coaching Tip

Leave them a message that's hard to ignore.

A: No matter how great your need is for those customers to call, it's their need to talk with you that determines the outcome. So the more you find out up front about their needs, problems, goals, and interests, the more you'll have to work with when you call to follow up. That's why it's important to spend time asking good questions before pushing to sell people.

When you do call again, what *won't* help is to let your frustration leak out into your messages. *"This is the sixth time I've called you this month"* or a similar voicemail message that echoes with resentment, self-pity, or anxiety will make you even more likely to be avoided. A little gentle humor would be a better way to acknowledge that you've called several times ("Hi, Jim, just hovering a little here, in search of a good time to touch base. Buzz you back later."). Offer the person easy options for how and when to get back to you, and try them again after another week.

What *will* help you get your calls returned is to leave a tantalizing message. A message blending elements of appreciation and curiosity is an irresistible attention grabber: "I appreciate what you've done. Please call back so I can thank you personally." The challenge is, how do you find a way to frame this for a prospective customer? Sales reps regularly scour the business news, for example, to find accomplishments on which they can congratulate the prospects they call. You will have to push the envelope to adapt this approach to your own prospects. Maybe a client posed a problem that led you to a brilliant new idea ("Jim, you planted a seed with me that really produced something great. You might want to hear about it, and I'd sure like to thank you if you'll give me a call back."). Just make sure you're prepared with an actual idea in case the customer calls back.

When Your Boss Springs Surprise Assignments

Q:

"My boss has a habit of dumping big projects on me at the last minute. She always makes some lame excuse about why she couldn't help it, but I suspect she just isn't very well organized. The upshot of all this is that I always seem to be working under a lot of pressure, which I hate. Is there any way I can encourage her to give me more notice?"

Coaching Tip

Ask not what your boss can do for you; ask if there's anything you can do for your boss.

A: Like secondhand smoke, secondhand stress can be hazardous to your health. Your boss's "catch-up" style has a negative impact on the quality of work you turn out as a team, as well as on your morale. You owe it to both of you to try making it easier for her to plan ahead.

Give her some feedback about the impact of her behavior. Find a relatively quiet time to talk with her and say something like

"I appreciate how swamped you are and I'd like to help you keep on top of things in any way I can. It concerns me that we end up with so many last-minute deadlines. I know that I do better work when I have more time to prepare. I have a few thoughts on how we might stay ahead of things. Would you be open to hearing them?"

In encouraging your boss to plan ahead, emphasize advantages to her, rather than dwelling on how the pressure is affecting you. Besides pointing out that you produce better work when you have more lead time, you can mention that more notice for you means more opportunity for her to critique your work and suggest improvements. Others awaiting your products (like your boss's boss) may also appreciate getting them earlier.

You might suggest a brief meeting with your boss at the start or end of each work week (whichever tends to be a less stressful time for her) for the purpose of reviewing what's coming up on the calendar and setting priorities and deadlines together. If your boss seems reluctant to agree to this, ask her if she'd be willing to try it for just a month, in order to see if it's useful.

When your boss reverts to her last-minute ways, try to keep your cool. Calmly let her know that you will do your best, and spell out the consequences of your having to shuffle your workload. Tell her which projects will need to be moved to the back burner in order for you to comply with her new demands, or ask her to clarify which items on your to-do list can be postponed.

Encouraging a "Computer-Phobic" Direct Report

Q:

"One of the supervisors who reports to me simply refuses to enter the modern age. He insists that he has no need to become computer literate and admits that computers make him uncomfortable. Instead, he writes reports and memos in longhand and gives them to the secretaries to type. No one else at his level operates this way, so it takes him longer to produce everything. People kid him about it, but it's a productivity issue. He's a valuable person and I want to help him get over this hump."

Coaching Tip

Respect people's fears without giving in to them.

A: Maybe he saw *2001: A Space Odyssey* as a kid, and he's still traumatized by memories of HAL, the homicidal computer. Well, seriously, . . . he's anxious. When we say that someone is "phobic," it means they're avoiding the thing they fear, which keeps them from overcoming their fear. Trying to force him or making fun of him will probably just increase his anxiety. Instead, you can work on increasing his motivation to change and support him in taking manageable steps forward.

Let him know that you value his work and offer some gentle feedback about how using the computer could help him become even more effective. Ask whether he sees any benefits at all (on or off the job) in developing some basic computer skills. Acknowledge that many people have irrational fears about using the computer. Ask him to share his fantasies about the worst thing that could happen if he tried to use it. Sometimes humor and paradox can help defuse anxiety: Does he think it might take over his brain?

Then provide an understanding guide to help him experiment with the computer in small doses. An all-day computer class right off the bat could blow him out of the water, but he might be able to spend half an hour on the computer three times a week with a supportive teacher by his side. Acknowledge his efforts in a low-key way that won't embarrass him ("Nice job on that memo, Dave."). Eventually he'll take his place on the information highway.

Making a Pitch for More Resources

Q:

"I have two vacant positions on my team that my boss hasn't allowed me to fill because of the economic downturn. As a result, we're at the end of our rope trying to keep up with customer demands. How can I convince my boss that it would make sense to fill those positions now?"

Coaching Tip

Hitch your wagon to your boss's star.

Ask yourself, "If filling those positions were my boss's idea, what would his or her reasoning be?" Consider all you know about your boss's goals, needs, and values and try to align your goal to his or her agenda. What are the long-term benefits your boss would see to hiring more staff? Would doing so give you a competitive edge or allow you to develop new services? Also, think about whether there are problems looming that could be avoided or alleviated by hiring new staff (such as retaining customers who might leave if you can't keep pace with their needs).

In addition to considering the big picture, develop a compelling rationale for hiring *now*. Are there immediate threats or opportunities to which your boss would want to respond? If adding staff would enable you to take on a specific new client, for example, your boss may be persuaded to give you a green light.

Look for ways to get a "foot in the door" by proposing a modest step your boss could agree to immediately. Could you hire one new person part-time and add hours as business picks up? Or would your boss approve undertaking some recruitment just to see what kinds of candidates are out there, with an okay to hire only if she or he is truly impressed with the search results? Another way to get a foot in the door might be to ask your boss to read a proposal that includes your revenue projections, based on the addition of staff.

Finally, let your boss see your enthusiasm for the proposal. Positive energy can be contagious.

Persuading Customers to Try a New Service

Q:

"Our financial consulting firm needs to develop new customers and expand services to our existing ones. I'm not a trained salesperson, and I'm not having much success persuading even my current clients to try some of our new services. I try to explain our programs clearly and give examples of how they'll help my clients, but so far it's strictly 'no sale.' How can I do better at this?"

 Coaching Tip

When you want to be persuasive, drop your agenda for a while.

A: It's a paradox that when we are most eager to "sell" somebody, that's the time to slow ourselves down. You're on the right track in showing your customers how they can benefit from your new services, but you'll be able to do this more effectively if you hold off your pitch and, instead, ask them questions to better understand their needs and concerns. You'll be more persuasive if you can tie the benefits of your programs directly to your customers' needs. And if you learn that it's not a match at present, you'll know enough to save the spiel (it's great that the health club you manage now has aerobic dancing, but don't pitch it to the member who just broke her ankle).

In addition to interviewing your customers before selling them, you can improve your effectiveness by finding ways to get a "foot in the door" rather than pushing for a decision right away. Examples of ways to do this are to give the customer some material to read, to suggest an experiment or pilot project, or to deal with a single issue, rather than the whole ball of wax, when you get resistance. Many plastic surgeons, for example, lure prospective patients with computer-simulated photos of how they'll look after cosmetic procedures, a very compelling foot (or nose, as the case may be) in the door.

It's also important to be patient and persistent with people you want to persuade. Give them time and space to mull over your proposal, but don't give up. Check in with them periodically in a friendly, low-key way. As circumstances change, so may their level of interest in your proposals. Approach them with phrases such as:

- ❏ "I'm calling to check in with you about . . ."
- ❏ "I was reviewing my notes from our last conversation and thought this might be a good time to . . ."
- ❏ "Last time we spoke, you were concerned about _____, and I wondered how things have been developing."

When a Colleague Thwarts Your Needs

Q:

"An opportunity just came up for me to go on a cruise with friends during the spring holidays. The problem is that a co-worker already got approval to take his vacation then. We're a small department, and our supervisor won't let both of us take off at the same time. If I'd asked first, I'd have gotten the time because I have seniority, but the boss won't reverse his decision now that he has approved the other person's request. The thing is, my co-worker isn't even going anywhere special; he's just spending the time with his family while his kids are on spring break. He doesn't even seem willing to compromise and share the time off. I hate to just give up. Any suggestions?"

Coaching Tip

When a conflict arises, start asking questions.

A: You and your colleague have competing goals, a difficult kind of conflict to resolve to both parties' satisfaction. Compromise usually means that each party gets something and each gives something in order to reach a resolution. Sometimes that results in a no-win situation, where neither is truly pleased with the outcome, which would seem to be the case if you divided the time. In contrast, a win-win solution is one in which both walk away happy. Easier said than done.

But before giving up, you can try to ferret out and understand everybody's needs and interests in this situation. So far, you know that your colleague puts a high premium on time with his family. Is it possible that there are upcoming holidays or occasions when it might be even more important for him to take time off to be with them? If so, can you cover for him then? What else, besides the current issue, is important to him? Can you offer anything to make his life easier on the job?

You can also explore with your supervisor what his or her concerns are about the two of you being off the same week. If you know more specifically what problems the supervisor anticipates, maybe you and your co-worker can put your heads together and propose some creative solutions.

Finally, talk with your friends about what's important to them in the situation. Are there compelling reasons for them to take the cruise at this particular time? If so, what are they? If they got a special deal, can you find a better one for a time that works out for you? Are weather conditions for their destination optimal in the spring, or would another season actually work out better for all of you? The Bermuda Triangle may be a bargain in hurricane season, but there's a good reason for that.

It's possible that some of this exploration on your part may produce proposals you can put forth in the negotiation process. If not, you will know that you tried. Either way, do your best to remain gracious with all the parties involved so that good relationships survive the conflict. This may at least help ensure that the next conflict has a chance to produce a win-win solution.

When You're Caught in the Middle

Q:

"An executive vice president has asked me to assist him with a project. It could be a great opportunity for me to demonstrate my advancement potential. The problem is, he hasn't cleared this with my boss and he's probably too busy to want to be bothered with doing so. And knowing my boss, she might think I'm going around her or scrimping on her assignments. What's the best way to handle the situation?"

Coaching Tip

It's usually better to get people to talk to each other than to interpret for them.

A: Don't be the monkey in the middle. When higher-ups violate the chain of command, you will be the one who suffers in the end. That's the nature of life on the organizational food chain.

How do you discourage bosses from upsetting the table of organization? Carefully. Obviously, you cannot order Mr. Executive VP to communicate his request directly to your boss, but you need to do what you can to induce him to do so. It's better for everyone if the bosses communicate with each other rather than through you. If you serve as intermediary, there will be a greater likelihood of some misunderstanding, for which (as low guy on the totem pole) you may be blamed.

So the two things you can do are to make it (1) advantageous and (2) convenient for the VP and your boss to get together on this. To address item 1, identify how it might benefit each of the bosses to communicate directly. For example, if the VP wants his project completed on time (and why wouldn't he?), you can say, "Maybe Susan can free me up from some of my existing projects if you explain to her why you want me to help." A benefit for Susan might be the chance to do a favor for her boss.

To make contact convenient, try to take on the role of administrative assistant and facilitate communication between the bosses. Rather than leave it open-ended ("So, you'll get in touch with Susan?"), offer to take immediate steps to link them:

❑ *"Susan's in the field, but I have her pager number. Would you like me to give her a call right now?"*

❑ *"Are there any convenient times this week that you could meet with Susan?"*

❑ *"Suppose I summarize all this in an e-mail to you and Susan so the two of you can follow up. Would that be helpful?"*

If the VP resists your efforts, remain pleasant and positive, but reiterate your expectation that your boss will have the opportunity to bless the decision ("I'll give Susan a heads-up that you'll be in touch, and I'm sure she'll call you if she has any questions.").

Strategy 6:
Think We, Not Me

The final strategy that will bring success involves your willingness to be *collaborative.* In today's workplace, a vital part of everyone's job description is to be a team player. The better you are at this "job," the more valuable you are to your organization.

Even if your current work situation involves mostly *independent* activity, what you do workwise still affects others and requires some level of concern for their welfare. If your current work situation involves mostly *interdependent* activity, then your ability to collaborate is essential.

Collaboration does not come easily. There are many circumstances in which you may be unaware of how you affect others. Without this knowledge, you may not even have a sense of what you can do to assist them. And even if you are aware of the kinds of collaboration that would be helpful, you may still be reluctant to extend yourself. Including others can be frustrating, and you may prefer to "do it yourself." Figuring out what others need can often require guesswork. Your motivation to be a team player may be diminished by feelings of annoyance or anger at the actions of others.

Teamwork is perhaps the most complicated work relationship—or should we say "relationships"? When you work with one other person, there's just one shared relationship. Add a third person, and the number of relationships jumps to six. Why? In addition to each person's relationship with each of the others (three relationships), each also has to deal with the alliance (or conflict) between the other two people in the group (a total of three more relationships). In a team of four people there are 24 linkages between group members, in a group of five there are 120, and in a team of six people there are 720 relationships going on! Each time a team is increased by one member, its complexity rises geometrically.

Because teams are like an interpersonal traffic jam, it is imperative to recognize that things take more time, processes go more slowly, and you sometimes have to be more patient about getting your own point across. Even a team composed of brilliant, socially adept individuals will face these constraints. By some estimates, it takes several months for any team to perform effectively. A long-term orientation is imperative.

Keeping this fact in mind, people-smart individuals understand that supporting the team concept requires a special perspective.

Each of us comes to a team with our own talents. People-smart individuals come with something else: the ability to blend their talents with the skills of others around them. We also come with our own ideas and preferences. People-smart individuals balance interest in what they are advocating with interest in what others are saying. They also see themselves and others as team resources rather than as individual egos. They act as if they are part of the team's pool of knowledge, skills, and ideas and are successful in getting others to act that way also. In essence, they think "we rather than me."

You can think "we rather than me" in everyday interactions with the people you work with. Here is a list of ten things to do, even if you rarely or never meet together as a group.

Ten Things Team Players Do

 ① Pitch in and assist others.

We each have our own job to do, but there may be moments when we can take the time to help others who are very busy or in need of our support in any way. Look for opportunities to lend a hand. Maybe you have a special talent or skill others need. Even if you don't, a helping hand is always appreciated.

 ② Reach out to quiet or new teammates or co-workers.

In any group there are people who are more reticent than others. If group members don't engage such people, it becomes even more difficult for them to open up and become part of the team. Look for opportunities to make these people feel included. Converse with them and seek their opinions. Invite them to join you for lunch or a coffee break. Ask them about their experiences. Find out what they need to be a part of the group and contribute to its success. Help them get to know you and others in the group.

3 Encourage teammates who are in conflict to talk out their differences.

One of the most valuable things you can do in any work group situation is to help people who are in conflict resolve their issues directly between themselves. Often a person will keep a safe distance from any squabbles among group members or allow one of the parties to vent and complain to him or her as a safe third party. Look for opportunities to encourage direct communication between the combatants. If someone approaches you to vent about another colleague, listen patiently but try to redirect the person's energy toward resolving the conflict.

4 Share the credit you receive for a job well done.

When public figures receive awards, they typically thank those who helped them achieve success. Such a gesture may come across as just a moment of modesty or social grace, but it doesn't have to be that way. Others usually deserve part of the credit. In work situations, the same requirement holds. When the credit is shared, the recipients feel appreciated and motivated to support your efforts in the future. Look for opportunities to acknowledge, both publicly and privately, the help and support you obtain from others.

5 Suggest team-building and problem-solving techniques.

Have you read, experienced, or received training in team-building techniques such as brainstorming, problem analysis, process checking, and consensus building? Any team tool you may know about may be very beneficial to the group you work with. It is not necessary to be the team leader to suggest a different process. Any member can do so. Look for opportunities where the group may benefit from a process you are familiar with.

6 Check to see how your decisions might affect others.

We often don't realize that a decision we make may negatively impact our colleagues. Review some recent decisions you have made and consider how they might affect others. Put yourself in their shoes. Do any of your decisions create inconvenience for others? Convey lack of interest or support? Lower morale? Cause new problems for others?

7 Include everyone in the information loop when appropriate.

No one needs to know everything you know or think. However, there are plenty of situations where information you have can be helpful or even essential to others. Even if, at first glance, the matter pertains only to you, consider whether your colleagues might benefit from this knowledge in the long run. Will it help them do their jobs better? Will the information help them to support your own job performance?

8 Seek information and expertise from others.

There are two reasons to seek the information and expertise of others: (1) Others may help you do your job better, and (2) others are recognized for the talents they bring to the team. Review tasks and assignments that you traditionally do by yourself and consider if the help of others will enhance your work. Take stock of the talents of others, especially when they are underutilized, and invite new contributions.

9 Communicate your own activity so that it is public knowledge.

Just as information and your private decisions often need to be shared for the sake of the team, simply letting others know about initiatives you have recently undertaken or events you have experienced may be important. Maybe you have encountered an interesting situation that could be shared. Maybe you are involved in a project or assignment that, if shared, would be of interest or benefit to your colleagues.

> **(10)** *Inform others what they can do to support your efforts, and ask them to tell you when they need help.*

This is the boldest collaborative action on this list. It is critical that colleagues know what you need from them to make you a happy team member and more effective contributor. Giving this feedback may feel awkward at first, but it gets easier to muster the courage once you've done it. Be sure to return the favor and ask others what you can do for them.

 Coaching Contract

Which of these ten actions do you undertake? How often? Which two would be the most valuable to do more often?

If you regularly meet as a group with your colleagues, there are additional steps you can take to contribute to the team's goals. Again, you do not have to be in a leadership position to do most of these things. As a mere group member, you can be extremely helpful.

Observe What's Going On in the Team

Many people in team situations are oblivious to what is happening around them. They are focused on themselves and fail to pick up cues about the situations of others. Perhaps someone has been excluded. Perhaps someone has a good idea but it's not being expressed well. Perhaps the team is on a tangent or caught up in debate when it should be brainstorming.

Here is a list of things you might watch for when your team meets.

❑ Does everyone have the same understanding of the team's goals? Does everyone support them?

❑ Do people seem free to express themselves?

❑ Do people listen to each other?

❑ Is there equal opportunity for participation?

❑ Is the team focused and energized?

❑ Are members in the team building on each other's ideas?

❑ Is conflict accepted and handled?

❑ Do team members know about each other's needs?

If the answer to any of these questions is no, share your observations with others. See if they agree. Seek some solutions.

Encourage Creative Problem Solving

A group's creativity is fostered by thinking "outside the box"—looking at issues in new ways and developing novel solutions to problems. Brainstorming is a well-known technique to free the imagination to come up with new ideas about goals, projects, solutions, or whatever. Most people assume that brainstorming is a "fast" process of getting as many ideas as possible in a very short period of time. However, brainstorming can be done at a leisurely pace as well.

Fast brainstorming can be compared to making popcorn. Kernels form in people's minds and out pop ideas (some of which may be corny). If things go well, you get a lot of ideas and then the process is exhausted. The process typically involves the following guidelines:

- ❏ Participants are urged to *go for quantity*. The more ideas, the better.

- ❏ Participants are encouraged to *think freely*. In some cases, the crazier the ideas, the better.

- ❏ Participants are invited to *toss out* ideas as they occur.

- ❏ Participants are required to *hold back any comments* about the ideas until the time for brainstorming is up.

As a result, the pace is usually frenzied and uninhibited.

Slow brainstorming has a different tempo and feel. Participants are expected to be thoughtful and responsive. As a result, fewer ideas might be developed, but perhaps the quality is improved. However, there are still "rules" that qualify it as a form of brainstorming:

- ❏ Participants are asked to *wait a few seconds* before shouting out their ideas.

- ❏ Participants are sometimes requested to *write down ideas* before making them public.

- ❏ Participants are sometimes required to *limit themselves* to one contribution each until everyone has contributed or passed.

- ❏ Participants are urged to *ask clarifying questions*. When an idea is offered by someone, others are "allowed" to seek more information about the idea–as long as they don't make it sound like a judgment. For example, you might ask, "How much do you estimate that will cost?" (in a friendly tone of voice), but you would not ask (rhetorically), "Don't you think that's expensive?"

- ❏ Participants are encouraged to *add to an idea* ("Maybe we could also . . .").

The keys to either type of brainstorming session, fast or slow, are creative imagination and open, nonjudgmental interaction. Of course, once the ideas have been generated–whether quickly or slowly–they must be listed, discussed, and evaluated. One way to quickly sort out the participants' reactions to the brainstormed ideas is to group them into these categories:

- ❏ *Keepers* (implement immediately)
- ❏ *Maybes* (promising enough to warrant serious consideration)
- ❏ *Hold-offs* (put aside for now)

Often, brainstorming new ideas is difficult because the size of the problem taxes the creative imagination of the group. One way to overcome this situation is to break the problem, issue, or goal down into its constituent parts and examine each part separately. Then participants can brainstorm ideas involving each part. Doing this will help to loosen up participants, and they may produce some truly novel and productive ideas.

As the meeting begins, state the problem, issue, or goal about which you want to have a brainstorming session. Next, ask the participants to think about all the elements or parts of the problem, issue, or goal *by breaking it down.* (Or you may do this analysis for them prior to the meeting.)

As an example, consider the planning of a successful fundraising race. These are some aspects of the project to be considered:

- ❏ A slogan
- ❏ The course to be run
- ❏ The length of the race
- ❏ A date for the race (Is Saturday better than Sunday? Rain date or no? Maybe a holiday weekend?)
- ❏ Prizes
- ❏ A deadline for entries
- ❏ Emergency services
- ❏ Publicity before, during, and after the race

Take each part and think about the alternatives. New ideas in each of the areas could be so powerful that next year's race could be a real winner; or it could change into a different kind of event and not a race at all, as a result of the planners looking at the project from a different perspective.

A third strategy to encourage creative problem solving employs a technique called *scenario thinking*. Participants are asked to set aside present realities and dream up a wide range of new possibilities.

Select an issue, problem, or creative project facing the group. For example, a group might be discussing employee morale, slackening attendance/participation, or customer service. Tell the group that you would like them to set aside their current concerns about "things the way they are" and to think about a range of future possibilities to resolve the issue, problem, or project. Prod your colleagues, for example, by saying, "Let's dream a little together. How could we expand our thinking about this?" Encourage participants to share their ideas by using the phrase(s)

- ❑ *"I wonder . . ."*
- ❑ *"What if . . ."*
- ❑ *"Maybe we . . ."*
- ❑ *"I have a dream that . . ."*
- ❑ *"If only we . . ."*
- ❑ *"I wish . . ."*
- ❑ *"Why can't we . . ."*

Help Build a Climate of Dialogue

We use the expression "everyone is entitled to his or her own opinion" when we want to support freedom of speech. However, there are social limits to this right in team situations. Too often, team discussion becomes a debate of my idea versus your idea. People advocate for the causes dear to their hearts, hoping to gain support from others. The climate becomes very politicized. By contrast, when a climate of dialogue exists, team members listen to each other, react to and build on each other's ideas, and look for and acknowledge real differences of opinion.

The purpose of dialogue is to expand ideas, not diminish them. Here are ways in which you can help to build a climate of dialogue:

- ❑ Ask questions to clarify what others are saying. Invite others to seek clarification of your ideas.
- ❑ Share what's behind your ideas. Reveal your assumptions and goals. Invite others to do so in kind.
- ❑ Ask for others to give you feedback about your ideas.
- ❑ Give constructive feedback about the ideas of others.
- ❑ Make suggestions that build on the ideas of others.
- ❑ Incorporate the ideas of others into your proposals.
- ❑ Find common ground among the ideas expressed in the team.
- ❑ Encourage others to give additional ideas beyond those already expressed.

Let's now take a look at how our advice plays out in situations that may occur in your workplace.

Getting the Team Spirit

Q:

"I don't get teams. Remember the old saying that a zebra is a horse designed by committee? That's how I see teams. They're inefficient and frustrating. I can get more accomplished on my own, so why bother with the hassle of working with others?"

Coaching Tip

We usually get the team we deserve.

A: To an extent, you are correct. Tasks often do take longer to accomplish in a group because there's so much going on among the players. Reaching consensus can require time and effort. Moreover, because our culture places a premium on individual accomplishment, many people tend to view teamwork as warm, fuzzy stuff left over from the Age of Aquarius. And there's no question that being a team player adds new responsibilities to one's job description.

In spite of all this, teams are a fact of life and always have been. We are born into groups, in the form of families, and work our way through life participating in a variety of group activities, ranging from sports teams to sororities to street gangs. For better or worse, humans are social animals.

In the modern workplace, teams may be more essential than ever as technology and specialization make it increasingly unlikely that anyone knows enough about everything to maintain a competitive edge. Teams expand the pool of knowledge, skills, ideas, and energy available to get the job done successfully. A cohesive team can be a source of support and camaraderie for its members (sorry if this sounds too touchy-feely). If you doubt that there's a particular thrill in team, as opposed to individual, accomplishment, picture the members of a baseball team that has just won the World Series.

In the final analysis, teams are not intrinsically good or bad. A dysfunctional and dispirited collection of people is a team that goes nowhere—and slowly, at that. For a team to shine, its members need to "think we" and act on it in the ways that we discussed in the list of the ten things team players do. So in the words of Magic Johnson, "Ask not what your teammates can do for you; ask what you can do for your teammates." Your spirit may become contagious.

When Team Members Lock Horns

Q:

"I've been assigned to a task force that was convened to recommend strategies to deal with several employee-related issues at our company. After attending two meetings, I've concluded that the group is a disaster. The members are all from different departments and have totally different points of view. All they do is argue. We adjourned the last meeting early after an hour of people yelling at each other. How can a group like this accomplish anything?"

Coaching Tip

Everyone's got baggage. The key to resolving conflict is to unpack it.

A: When a team is deadlocked by conflict, it can be a painful and frustrating experience for everyone involved. As long as group members keep advocating for their own positions, the group will remain stuck. However, whether you are the group leader or one among equal group members, there are some facilitative interventions you can employ.

One helpful step would be to acknowledge the conflict. To do this, you summarize in neutral terms what the disagreements are. When you do this accurately, people begin to feel that they're being heard and can at least agree on the description of their conflict. Try saying something like "I guess it's clear to all of us that we have very different vantage points. Maybe we need to better understand each department's issues before we look for a general solution." The next step is to help members move beyond their stated positions and share their underlying needs and concerns. Invariably, people bring hidden agendas and issues to the negotiating table. Successful conflict resolution involves surfacing these concerns and incorporating them into the discussion. By "expanding the pie" in this manner, you increase the potential for creative problem solving. Also, when the parties in a conflict make an effort to understand each other, it brings good faith to the negotiating process.

The way to surface underlying issues is to ask good questions. In your task force, for example, it might be a good idea to give each member five minutes, in turn, to describe how the personnel issues have played out in their division while the other members listen without interrupting. When everyone has had a turn, push for a deeper understanding of their concerns by asking questions like

- ❑ *"How is this issue affecting morale and productivity in your division?"*
- ❑ *"What do you think will happen if the situation continues?"*
- ❑ *"What's the most important concern you have about the situation?"*
- ❑ *"How could the situation be improved?"*

❑ *"What else is important to your people?"*

❑ *"How would you say your unit's needs are similar to or different from those of the other divisions?"*

As group members gain more understanding of each other's circumstances, they can begin to brainstorm solutions more effectively.

When People Don't Participate Equally

Q:

"Within the team I lead, some members are quiet during meetings, while others tend to monopolize the discussion. I wouldn't feel comfortable just telling people to shut up, or trying to interrogate the quiet ones. Is there anything I can do to encourage more even participation?"

 Coaching Tip

Help group members share the microphone.

A: When some members monopolize the discussion, the more reticent ones may tend to give up. And the quieter they are, the more the monopolizers talk to fill the empty space–a vicious cycle. Here are some strategies that can be helpful:

❑ When seeking reactions or opinions, try asking, "How many of you have some thoughts on this subject?" Usually several people will raise their hands. You can then say, "I'd like to hear three people's views," thus expressing the expectation that others besides the monopolizer will respond.

❑ Vary the discussion formats to elicit participation. Use "go-arounds" to capture brief input from each member, or assign people to partners or subgroups to discuss an issue and report back to the larger group. You might also use index cards to gather opinions prior to a group discussion in order to elicit ideas from everyone.

❑ Set ground rules that may be ongoing or temporary. Suggest, "I'd like to see everyone feeling free to share their ideas and people making it a practice to hear each other out without interruption." Or vary the usual group process by announcing that, for the next fifteen minutes, no one is to speak twice until everyone who wishes to speak has had a chance to do so.

❑ When someone does monopolize, listen actively. Interject a brief summary of what he or she is saying and then ask for other opinions. If someone continues to hog the microphone, meet with him or her privately to discuss the issue. Enlist his or her help in your goal of getting the quiet people to speak up.

When Everybody Is on Overload

Q:

"Everyone in my department is so overloaded that it's impossible to get them to cooperate on projects, give input, or come to meetings. I actually hear people complain that they don't have time to go to the bathroom! Is there anything I can do to get their participation when I really need it?"

Coaching Tip

Make it easy for others to assist you.

A: It is difficult to collaborate when people are stretched so thin. And the worst thing you can do is show your annoyance and make them feel even more pressured.

You can maximize your chances of gaining their support by using a variety of strategies, such as these:

Set priorities. Avoid being like the boy who cried "wolf," sending out false alarms about your needs. Make sure it's a situation where others' input is really important and needed before you ask.

Keep key players informed. If you make a point of keeping those who have a stake in your activities up to date about what you're doing, they may be more willing and able to enter the picture when their input is needed. Brief e-mail messages that don't require a response can accomplish this.

Make it easy for them to respond. Request the least time- and effort-consuming input from your teammates. Don't ask for a meeting if a phone call will do the trick. When you communicate a problem or question via e-mail, list some possible solutions for their consideration if you can.

Tune in to WIFM. Figure out how they will benefit from assisting you and spell it out for them.

Reciprocate. Show your genuine appreciation when people do make the time to contribute. When you can, go out of your way to help them, in turn.

Finally, show understanding when people are just too busy to assist you. Acknowledge them by saying, "I know you'd help if you could. Maybe another time."

Coping with Turnover

Q:

"We've had so much turnover that we might as well have a revolving door leading to our department. It's very hard for a team to be productive in the face of so much upheaval. What can we do to make the best of the situation?"

 Coaching Tip

Change is part of business as usual.

A: Frequent turnover does take its toll on a team. All groups go through a developmental cycle, moving through the stages of forming, storming, norming, and performing. When key members leave and new ones enter, the group has to back up and reconstitute itself, bringing new people into the process and in turn accommodating to their different styles and contributions. There's no real quick fix for the problem, but there are a few ways to help the group stay healthy and functional while it goes through its recycling process. Here are some suggestions:

Carve out roles for stability. Rituals provide structure and tradition in groups (picture Dad carving the turkey at Thanksgiving). One way to preserve tradition in a group is to use an "effective committee" model and assign roles that members will fill during meetings (e.g., a meeting manager to run the session, a recorder to take notes, a timekeeper, and perhaps a facilitator who acts as process observer and helps the group shift gears when necessary). New members can quickly become familiar with these roles, and the model helps the group operate effectively while it goes through changes.

Take time to get acquainted. Icebreakers and other activities can be used periodically to help members get to know each other. Such activities can range from creative introductions (e.g., pairing people off and having them introduce their partners, or putting together a group resume) to more in-depth experiences, conducted in meetings or retreats, designed to help members get to know each other well, and even learn new things about people they've been working with for a while. For a slew of ideas for such activities, check out *101 Ways to Make Meetings Active* (Silberman, 1999, San Francisco: Pfeiffer, Chapter 6).

Mix and match members. People often "bond" and learn to work with each other in small, ad hoc groups. By assigning subgroups to time-limited projects, or even breaking into small groups during a regular team meeting to tackle different aspects of a problem, people get an opportunity to work more closely and learn each other's styles. As a variation, it might help to assign all newcomers to the department a "buddy" in the form of a colleague who's been around for a while. The buddy helps the new arrival to get oriented and to learn the customs and procedures, provides support, and answers questions to ease his or her transition into the department.

These are some of the ways to help groups work in the face of turnover. And to tell the truth, they even help teams that *aren't* facing turnover.

Getting a Team to Think Out of the Box

Q:

"As leader of a project team, how can I encourage my colleagues to contribute new ideas? I'm not the boss, and I probably couldn't order them to think out of the box even if I were. What are some ways to jog them out of their shyness, apathy, or resistance?"

Coaching Tip

Sometimes teams are like salad dressings. They're better if you shake them before using.

A: Even good teams can get caught in a rut. Fortunately, there are lots of strategies you can use to help them tap into their creative potential. Instead of launching into "meeting as usual" mode, try some of these methods of stimulating discussion and problem solving:

Warm them up. Use icebreakers and warm-up activities to engage and enliven team members before getting down to the business at hand. Getting a little wacky can help people get unstuck, so don't be afraid to introduce some humor. You might invite the group to start by brainstorming the best ways to wreck the meeting, inventing new uses for everyday objects, or developing quick scripts for a team commercial.

Change the room. Move the furniture, adjust the lighting, serve refreshments (or *different* refreshments).

Brainstorm. Invite members to use a variety of brainstorming techniques to generate new ideas. Brainstorming can be done quickly or slowly, verbally or using anonymous cards, or even on large "graffiti sheets" posted around the room.

Vary discussion methods. Large-group discussions are the staple of meetings. Vary the pace by experimenting with alternatives such as having subgroups debate the pros and cons of a proposal; using fishbowl designs (where some members discuss while others observe and possibly share feedback or observations); or rotating members through dyads, trios, or quartets to hold brief discussions on selected questions.

Dull meetings lead to dull thinking. By injecting new energy and fun, you can tap your team's vitality and spirit of collaboration.

Collaborating with Other Departments

Q:

"In our large organization, my work group is forced to depend on other units for supplies, services, and information we need to do our jobs. Sometimes this is like pulling teeth. Other times, it's like having our own teeth pulled! When another department doesn't cooperate and doesn't seem to care about our needs and priorities, how can we possibly collaborate?"

 Coaching Tip

Treat other departments like most-favored nations.

Sounds like one big, happy, dysfunctional family. Or a collection of sovereign nation-states, with their own ideologies and manifest destinies. And, in a way, this is true. Even though you are all under the same organizational umbrella, departments evolve their own cultures, perspectives, and ways of operating. It's better to accept this reality than to keep hitting your head against it.

When you need to build bridges to another work group, here are some helpful strategies:

Appoint an ambassador. Intergroup collaboration is enhanced when there is an effective liaison relationship. Designate someone from your team to interface with a counterpart in the other group. Choose someone with good interpersonal skills and the motivation to take the necessary time to build trust and communication. A good liaison is someone you can count on to give you reliable information about what's really going on with the other group.

Walk in their shoes. Try to see through the eyes of the other group, instead of complaining about their indifference. Identify their goals and concerns by asking questions and observing how they operate. If there is another department that seems to be working successfully with this group, consult them about what might be helpful.

Appreciate similarities and differences. Acknowledge and respect the ways in which the other department differs from yours, but look for common ground. In dealing with the other group, emphasize common interests and seek out ways you might compensate for or offset each other's weaknesses (for instance, by sharing technical knowledge or expertise).

When Your Staff Are in Conflict

Q:

"Two of my direct reports are constantly at odds with each other. The tensions between them are obvious to others on the team, and it's becoming a problem. How can I get them to work things out with each other?"

Coaching Tip

Be hard on the issues and soft on the people.

A: You have two main objectives here: to communicate your expectation that they find a way to collaborate, and to help them surface and resolve the issues that are preventing this. It would be a good idea to talk with each of them individually first. Explain that you are concerned that their conflicts are becoming a distraction for the team, and ask each to share his or her views and concerns about what's going on. Listen and try to objectively summarize what you're hearing. Conclude the meetings by thanking them each for their openness. Let them know that you want to help them iron this out and will be bringing them together to help facilitate that process.

Then meet with them together. Start by acknowledging that they've been having issues with each other which you've discussed and about which you have some understanding. Clearly reiterate your expectation that they work through these issues to achieve some level of collaboration and spell out what that will look like (e.g., they'll hear each other out without interrupting or making disparaging remarks in meetings, they'll co-write reports, they'll represent each other to clients in positive terms, etc.). Then share your impression of the conflict they are experiencing and identify what some of the key issues appear to be:

> *"It seems to me that you two often disagree about how to work with the support staff. Ben seems to like to delegate whenever possible, while Bob, you seem to prefer a more hands-on approach. But when you have to work as a team, the support staff end up with conflicting messages."*

Be descriptive, and don't label or cause either one to lose face. Then facilitate a discussion of what each of them needs–from each other and, perhaps, from you–to improve the situation. If things begin to get heated, restate calmly that you expect them to work this out. If things begin to overheat, call a time out and ask that each of them give further thought to how the situation can be improved before you reconvene the discussion. Acknowledge any helpful efforts on their parts to reach a resolution.

When an action plan is reached, note it in writing. After a brief period, reconvene to check on how the plan is going and to share any feedback you can give.

Now What?

At the beginning of this book, we promised to share with you "the know-how you require to sharpen your people edge." We also urged you to "take these strategies to work with you."

We hope you are inspired to apply our coaching suggestions back on the job. We recognize, however, that inspiration doesn't ensure action. So, as your coaches, we would like to end with some final advice and a concrete list of actions you might want to undertake to incorporate the six strategies for success into your job.

Making a Difference

Throughout this book, we have highlighted the theme that you can make a difference in your organization if you take the six strategies to heart. You have the opportunity to rise above the business-as-usual norms for working with others. Far too often, people in organizations tolerate, in themselves and in others, behaviors that shut down rather than open up communication, create tension rather than defuse it, and leave struggling co-workers to "shape up or ship out." If you are curious about others, if you include them in conversations, if you are honest about what you feel and want, if you seek their feedback, if you are open to their concerns, and if you are a team player, then you will set an example for others to follow and respond to in kind. As a result, you will enjoy being a vital part of a people-smart organization in which people bring out the best in each other. When that happens, the organization is bound to become more successful as well.

There is some risk, but the potential rewards—for yourself and for your organization—are worth it. You can make a difference if you are willing to

- ❑ Want it
- ❑ Learn it
- ❑ Try it
- ❑ Live it

Wanting It. Ask yourself if you are truly happy with the current state of people affairs in your organization. Do you want to accept the status quo, where the actions of others make you confused, crazy, or even angry? Do you want yourself to be a contributor to the people problems that abound rather than someone who helps to resolve them? It would be great if there were a magic wand that would dust (or inoculate) every one of us with the interpersonal courage to take the risks necessary to rise above the fray. But it doesn't exist. Are you willing to show some courage?

Learning It. It's one thing to be motivated to take action. It's another matter to do so intelligently. We hope you have learned or relearned some important interpersonal lessons from this book and, perhaps, from our first book, *PeopleSmart: Developing Your Interpersonal Intelligence.* You'll also find many other sources of interpersonal wisdom in a good bookstore or library. Studying the what, why, when, and how of effective people skills is necessary to your development as a person who brings out the best in others.

Trying It. We are often reluctant to change our interpersonal habits because we don't know what will happen if we do. View your attempts to apply the six strategies in this book as a "personal experiment in change." Exercise some new interpersonal muscles, and see if you become stronger and more gifted at dealing with others. Choose one experiment at a time and stay with it for a week. Try the new behavior "on for size" and see if it fits you. Shortly, we will give you a dozen experiments to try. Go for it!

Living It. If any of your experiments in change brings success, you're likely to continue practicing it for a while. However, the bumps and bruises of life intervene, and we are all prone to relapse. Recognize those barriers that get the best of your resolve, and think about what you need to do to overcome them. Maybe you need to obtain some support from others. Maybe you need to go back to what got you motivated in the first place to start the journey of change. They say, "Nobody likes a change except a wet baby!" Prove them wrong. You can make a difference as long as you commit yourself over the long haul.

Twelve Experiments in Change

Following are a dozen "experiments in change." Look them over and select one that appeals to you. Try it out. You might even tell someone else what your plan is. See if you like the results. If you do, select others—but one at a time! Eventually, you'll see how good you're getting at working people-smart.

 Looking below the surface.

Think of someone you simply don't understand at all. Think about this person's behavior in a few key situations. Do his or her actions reflect the person's anxieties? Is the person concerned about *control, connection,* or *competence*? When you view the person as anxious rather than difficult, do you understand him or her better? In light of this insight, consider how you might change your own behavior toward this person and try it out for a week. See if changing tactics makes a difference.

 Understanding differences.

Identify someone at work who's as different as possible from you. On a 1 to 10 scale, where 1 is the lowest and 10 the highest rating, rate how well you understand this person's values, assumptions, and motivation. Now list some of the ways in which this person differs from you, including goals, personal style, gender, age, and cultural background. Which of these differences may be interfering with your ability to understand this person? Try to imagine yourself as this person, seeing the world through his or her eyes. Do this for one week. What happens?

 Checking for understanding.

Practice confirming understanding for a week. Whenever you've talked at length or introduced a complicated subject, make a point of checking out the listener's understanding by asking questions such as "Was that clear?" or "Do you have any questions about what I'm saying?" You might also check out this person's reactions to what you are communicating by asking, "What do *you* think about _____?" Observe what happens when you make a habit of checking for understanding and obtaining reactions.

④ Giving assignments.

Choose a new assignment you want to give someone. Think carefully how you would explain the task to that person *as if you had never done it before.* Then go ahead and talk with that person, keeping in mind that he or she is your "communication partner." Note whether your attempts to include the person lead to better understanding and execution.

⑤ Being straightforward.

For a few days, keep a record of situations at work in which you were not up front with someone else–when you hinted and hedged, but didn't say what was on your mind. Or you brought up a subject other than the one you really wanted to raise. Think about the reasons you were evasive. Select one or two situations that might arise again and plan how you can be more straightforward. Then try out your plan and see how it goes.

⑥ Making clear requests.

Review the requests you want to make of others to help you meet your own needs at work. Select one or two. Get clear in your mind what you specifically want. Formulate each request so that it is as reasonable as possible for the person you will ask, and then make your request(s). Did you get a positive response? Are you happy with the support you obtained? If so, try to make other clear requests, where appropriate.

7 Requesting feedback.

Identify someone from whom you'd like to get feedback. Approach the person and say, "I'd like to improve my . . . *(select a quality, skill, or behavior)*. Could you tell me how well I'm doing right now, and also let me know in the future if there's any change for the better or worse? Could we set a time to do this?" Evaluate the results.

8 Giving feedback.

Select two people to whom you'd like to give feedback, even if you're not sure they want it. Select one of them to whom you have never given feedback, or haven't done so in a long time. Think carefully about what you will say that would be constructive for that person, and then find an opportunity to do so. What were the results? Move on to giving feedback to the other person. Are you getting more confident?

9 Surfacing concerns.

Think of a person who resists a suggestion or recommendation you have given. Consider if you have done enough to explore that person's concerns or objections. Devote a week to working on asking that person questions rather than giving him or her your advice. Learn more about the person's needs, preferences, and wishes, and build trust. See if the person is becoming more open to your suggestion or recommendation.

10 Brainstorming solutions.

Choose a current conflict situation and brainstorm as many options as you can to resolve it so that each party achieves some measure of satisfaction. Do you think any of these solutions might be workable? Share your list with the other party and invite the person to add his or her own ideas. How did this win-win approach work?

11 Identifying teamwork opportunities.

Make a list of things you do independently of others at work. Examine the list and identify items where it would be helpful if you involved others rather than doing things alone. Plan how to include their assistance and expertise. See how you and the others benefit.

12 Improving your team's meetings.

Think about how your work team solves problems and makes decisions. Do powerful members express their preferences, with everyone else simply going along? Talk up the advantages of brainstorming and reaching decisions by consensus. Listen to people's concerns about the time required and other issues. Suggest ways in which these concerns can be alleviated.

As you undertake any of these experiments, be your own coach, because now it's up to you to work people-smart.

Index

About the Authors

Mel Silberman, Ph.D.

Mel Silberman is a psychologist known internationally as a pioneer in the areas of interpersonal intelligence, active learning, and facilitation/consultation. As Professor of Adult and Organizational Development at Temple University, Mel has won two awards for his distinguished teaching. He is also President of Active Training, Princeton, New Jersey, a provider of products, seminars, and publications in his areas of expertise. He has more than thirty-five years of experience in creating and honing techniques that inspire people to be people-smart, to learn faster, and to collaborate effectively.

Mel shares his original and practical ideas throughout his books, and through active training programs and customized seminars for corporate, educational, human services, and governmental organizations. His training skills, psychological insights, and engaging personality have made him a popular speaker at conferences of the American Society for Training and Development, the International Society for Performance Improvement, the Society of Human Resource Management, and the North American Simulation and Gaming Association.

Among his numerous publications are

PeopleSmart: Developing Your Interpersonal Intelligence

Active Training: A Handbook of Techniques, Designs, Case Examples, and Tips

Active Learning: 101 Strategies to Teach Any Subject

101 Ways to Make Training Active

101 Ways to Make Meetings Active

The Best of Active Training

The Consultant's Tool Kit

Mel is also Editor of *The Training and Performance Sourcebook* and *The Team and Organization Development Sourcebook,* both leading annual collections.

Freda Hansburg, Ph.D.

Freda Hansburg is co-author of *PeopleSmart* and Vice President of Active Training. She is also a psychologist in private practice, an executive coach, and a training consultant whose recent clients include BMW of North America, Depository Trust and Clearing Corporation, Merck, and Valero Refining. She has also contributed to *The Training and Performance Sourcebook* and given presentations about interpersonal intelligence for ASTD and the OD Network. Freda is the former director of the Technical Assistance Center, a behavioral health consultation and training program at the University of Medicine and Dentistry of New Jersey.

PeopleSmart Products and Services

PeopleSmart is a comprehensive provider of seminars, workshops, coaching services, and training tools that sharpen the people skills most critical to organizational success. Its network of consultant partners work closely with organizations to find solutions for their specific needs. Recent clients include BMW of North America, Chevron, Consolidated Edison, Depository Trust and Clearing Corporation, Dow Chemical, Great Clips, John Deere, Linens N' Things, Merck, MGM Grand, PA Office of Mental Retardation, Pfizer, Philadelphia Workforce Development Corp., Procter & Gamble, Quadrix Solutions, Select Comfort, Starkey Laboratories, Valero Refining, Virtua Health, and Wyeth BioPharma.

Programs

Working PeopleSmart, our flagship small-group seminar, available for leaders, associates and intact teams

The 6 PeopleSmart Strategies for Success, a six-hour motivational workshop

The PeopleSmart How-to Series, targeted sessions on selected topics

PeopleSmart Coaching, individual support, feedback, and action planning for leaders who want to enhance their interpersonal performance and problem solving

The PeopleSmart Training Institute, an intensive seminar for trainers who want to enhance their own talents to design and facilitate interpersonal skills training using the PeopleSmart model.

The PeopleSmart Coaching Institute, an intensive seminar for professionals who provide coaching services for leaders, focusing on interpersonal skills development

Products

PeopleSmart: Developing Your Interpersonal Intelligence: The book that delivers a powerful plan for making your relationships more productive and rewarding by developing your interpersonal intelligence

Developing Your PeopleSmart Skills: A series of handbooks addressing the eight competencies of interpersonal intelligence: Understanding People, Asserting Your Needs, Influencing Others, Being a Team Player, Expressing Yourself Clearly, Exchanging Feedback, Resolving Conflict, and Changing Tactics

Working PeopleSmart Video and Leader's Guide: On-camera interviews with the authors of *PeopleSmart*, outlining the eight essential PeopleSmart skills (includes 67-page Leader's Guide)

www.activetraining.com
800-924-8157
info@activetraining.com

Do You Work People-**Smart?**

If you have had success bringing out the best in your colleagues, customers, direct reports, or your boss, tell us about it!

We are looking for success stories to publish in our next book. Share with us whatever you have . . . from a quick suggestion to a detailed account of how you utilized the six strategies for success to open up communication, defuse tensions, or actually help to change someone else's behavior.

Be a contributor to our campaign to influence how we work together . . . in a people-smart way.

Send to: info@activetraining.com

PeopleSmart
Developing Your Interpersonal Intelligence

Mel Silberman, Ph.D., with Freda Hansberg, Ph.D.

Everyone is in the people business, because all of us deal with other people all the time. That's why it's smart to reap the benefits of this eminently practical guide. *PeopleSmart* details the eight essential skills of interpersonal intelligence and provides a powerful plan for becoming more effective in every relationship—with supervisors, coworkers, a spouse, family, and friends.

Paperback original • ISBN 1-57675-091-4 • Item #50914 $18.95

Developing Your PeopleSmart Skills
A Handbook Series

This booklet series makes the invaluable lessons of the book *PeopleSmart* available in an inexpensive and easily distributed format.

Asserting Your Needs • ISBN 1-58376-160-8 • Item #61608
Being a Team Player • ISBN 1-58376-164-0 • Item #61640-
Changing Tactics • ISBN 1-58376-165-9 • Item #61659-
Exchanging Feedback • ISBN 1-58376-161-6 • Item #61616
Expressing Yourself Clearly • ISBN 1-58376-159-4 • Item #61594
Influencing Others • ISBN 1-58376-162-4 • Item #61624
Resolving Conflict • ISBN 1-58376-163-2 • Item #61632
Understanding People ISBN 1-58376-158-6 • Item #61586

Each booklet: paperback, 32-48 pages, $7.95

Getting Things Done When You Are Not In Charge

Second Edition

Geoffrey M. Bellman

Geoff Bellman offers practical guidance for all of us who are not in charge on how to make a difference in our organizations and accomplish our own goals while supporting the work of others. This new edition of the international bestseller has been streamlined and thoroughly updated with new material.

Paperback • ISBN 1-57675-172-4 • Item #51724 $15.95

Berrett-Koehler Publishers
PO Box 565, Williston, VT 05495-9900
Call toll-free! **800-929-2929** 7 am-9 pm EST
Or fax your order to 1-802-864-7626
For fastest service order online: **www.bkconnection.com**

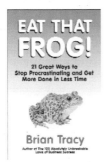

Berrett-Koehler books are available at quantity discounts for orders of 10 or more copies.

Working PeopleSmart
6 Strategies for Success

Mel Silberman, Ph.D.
and Freda Hansburg, Ph.D.

Paperback original
ISBN 1-57675-208-9
Item #52089 $18.95

To find out about discounts for orders of 10 or more copies for individuals, corporations, institutions, and organizations, please call us toll-free at (800) 929-2929.

To find out about our discount programs for resellers, please contact our Special Sales department at (415) 288-0260; Fax: (415) 362-2512. Or email us at bkpub@bkpub.com.

Subscribe to our free e-newsletter!
To find out about what's happening at Berrett-Koehler and to receive announcements of our new books, special offers, free excerpts, and much more, subscribe to our free monthly e-newsletter at www.bkconnection.com.

Berrett-Koehler Publishers
PO Box 565, Williston, VT 05495-9900
Call toll-free! **800-929-2929** 7 am-9 pm EST

Or fax your order to 1-802-864-7626
For fastest service order online: **www.bkconnection.com**